Painter Nguyễn Gia Trí's Words on Creation:
Notes Kept by Nguyễ Xuân Việt

by

Nguyễ Xuân Việt

DORRANCE
PUBLISHING CO
EST. 1920
PITTSBURGH, PENNSYLVANIA 15238

Dorrance Publishing Co
585 Alpha Drive
Pittsburgh, PA 15238
Visit our website at *www.dorrancebookstore.com*

ISBN: 978-1-6480-4257-7
eISBN: 978-1-6470-2600-4

Jung, Carl G Collected Works. Vol. 9. Part 1

Archetypes and the Collective Uncons—

C. ins. Pantheon $7.50

Jung C. G & W. Pauli Interpretation of Nature

and the Psyche Pantheon $3.00

Jung, C. G. Symbols of Transformation R— $5.00

In memory of painters

V. Tardieu

J. Inguimberty

the two so devoted French teachers of great Vietnamese painters.

BY WAY OF FOREWORD

I have had the chance to meet with painter Nguyễn Gia Trí a few years before he passed away, or as he used to say: "Sleep a sound sleep, to see oneself recovering consciousness the following morning".

The reason for which I have got that chance was that we wished to restore the painting entitled "Nativity" he had realized in 1941[1]. I was shown the way to the house of the Master by artist Thanh Liêm. I met him in a modest house, that doesn't look like the residence of a great Master. I didn't find any painting or any of his own works there. At present, after going through the work entitled: "Painter Nguyễn Gia Trí's Words on Creation" by artist Nguyễn Xuân Việt, the favourite and faithful disciple of the Master. I've understood the reason why he didn't want to keep anything for himself.

---

(1) This painting is now exposed at the church of the Dominican order, at No.44 Tú Xương Street, District 3, Hồ Chí Minh City.

Indeed, through this book that transcribes words and sentences that seem to have neither head nor tail, quite similar to the ones in the Analects, or to be more precise, that resemble to the words of a Zen master, we can see that painter Nguyễn Gia Trí isn't simply a well-known painter, but he's also a Taoist priest, or we can say, without being cantankerous, that he's a genuine Zen master. Painting for him is only a means to reach the True Path. He once said: *"One must always remember that one's paintings constitute only a means to cultivate moral conduct and to train oneself"*, and *"a painting is like a raft for crossing a river that must be discarded after the crossing; without a raft, one can walk on foot"*.

Through his painting work, painter Nguyễn Gia Trí turns into a Taoist priest, by means of cultivating moral conduct and training himself to reach the *"non –ego"*, as, according to him, *"art begins only when one reaches one's non-ego"*. While *"Art knows no-want, and similarly, when one doesn't want anything, one knows no bondage, so one's heart is at peace, pure, and clean"*. Therefore *"cultivating moral conduct is aimed at reaching something transcendental"*, as the Master once said: *"Art knows no-want, and as it knows no – want, it's ascending towards something extremely high"*.

But what is meant by taking to religion? Painter Trí said: *"Taking to religion means returning to one's source,*

*to the source of the "Cam Lồ" (Holywater) to drink, so that
one can maintain oneself in constant youth and freshness".*

While reading the above–mentioned lines, I get the
impression that I'm reading Laozi or a certain Zen master
such as Bodhidharma or Tuệ Trung Thượng Sĩ. The only
difference is that painter Nguyễn Gia Trí reaches the True
Path through his painting art. While painting,he has become
a hermit by means of forgetting himself in his paintings,
i.e. reaching a *"non-ego"* state, reaching the *"void-nothingness"*. He said: *"A good painter must be able to paint
the "void-nothingness"*. And he unbosomed himself: *"I
worked in lacquer since it first appeared, so it has almost
the same age with mine. I live with it like a fish with water,
so I no longer feel that I'm living my life. Only other people
know that I'm living it"*. Painter Nguyễn Gia Trí has indeed reached *"nothingness"*, *"nonaction and quietness"*,
as well as *"non-ego"*. Here, we recall the story of the ancient Chinese philosopher Zhuang Zhu who dreamed of
being transformed into a butterfly, and didn't know whether
he was the butterfly or the butterfly was himself.

Being determined to take to religion, painter Nguyễn
Gia Trí had to accept loneliness. He confided: *"A talented
artist is practically always lonesome. It's a quite rare thing
to have an intimate friend"*. He also dealt much with the
desert. He said: *"To cleanse one 's soul of all stains, one
has to go into the desert"*, and *"entering the desert to secure a brand - new mind"*.

213

Painter Nguyễn Gia Trí's desire to remain *"young"* and *"fresh"* makes us think of the advocacy of being a "new-born child" of Laozi, and Jesus' invitation: *"If you don't become similar to a newborn child, it will be difficult for you to enter the Kingdom of Heaven"*.

The artist's mind is always young and fresh as the artist is constantly on his way looking for the new, and discovering unknown worlds, as in painter Nguyễn Gia Trí's words: *"Art is a means for us to enter unknown worlds"*. Such unknown worlds are also the ones religion is in search of.

Therefore, according to him, *"The painting art is close to religion as it emanates from man's heart. It isn't made out of brain or hand"*. Otherwise *"It's because of religion that man has a value. And, it's also thanks to religion that art is valuable"*. And he added: *"Everything is false, except for the Way"*. For that reason, he always turned to that ultimate truth. Painting is for practising his religion, and practising his religion is for reaching the Way. Painting is living up to his religion, as *"In ordinary life, painting and prayers have a close relation"*. Painter Nguyễn Gia Trí's way is something *"natural"*, something *"as light as a breath, requiring no effort"*.

He said: *"Just work in a natural way, without laying any plan, and one is conformable to the Way"*. However, that *"natural"* state isn't this natural and materalistic world, but it's a natural state leading to the preternatural. He said: *"Only after reaching a natural state, can one think of elevating oneself to a preternatural one"*, and *"the main thing is to retain one's naturally kind disposition, and to preserve oneself from being materialized"*.

In our present tumultuous and agitated world, a world in which mankind is more and more subsiding and becoming materialized, painter Nguyễn Gia Trí's paintings and mind can be considered as significant emblems of our national culture which we're proudly setting off.

Painter Nguyễn Gia Trí is not only a master painter, he also deserves to be considered as a venerable hermit we all ought to hold in high esteem and to honour. And, as a matter of fact, his Buddhist name "Thiện Chân" (Upright and Truthful) has fully justified what people used to say: *"The fame well suits the man"*.

July 3, 1995
Revd Father Thiện Cẩm

The TAO that can be told is not the eternal Tao.
The name that can be named is not the eternal name.

Lao Tzu

It's difficult to find one's mind
Spread, it covers the universe
Reduced, it is not larger than the point of a needle

Bodhidharma

The main lines of the Great Learning consist of:
illuminating one's high virtues, causing one's people
to continually innovate and cease at the best virtuousness.

Confucius

KEEPING NOTE OF PAINTER NGUYỄN GIA TRÍ'S WORDS ON CREATION

1975 - 1992

June 1, 1975

Keep on with painting, paint whatever one might meet with. Paint fastly, so as to catch up one's emotion.[1]

One must train one's eyes to see, to perceive beauty. To paint how to create life, a life which is green and beautiful as flowers and plants.

Were we to fail to have our own emotion and to create, then no one can help us to create.

November 14, 1975

Transparency must exist between creation and life, and must constitute a mutual sympathy. Life incites us to paint, just like a tree must absorb light and water to feed its leaves and to bloom.

---

1. Painter Nguyễn Sáng once told me: "If you want to paint, paint immediately..." According to Miro: Painting emotion is also a poetical emotion. Painting means writing poems with figures, colours, strokes... Picasso also said: "Nowadays there are so many painters who forget poetry in their paintings - while poetry is the most important thing". (All footnotes belong to artist Nguyễn Xuân Việt).

Simply reject all ancient and archaic prejudices. Paint with a completely new mind. It's the conventional fixed ideas that destroy art.

Don't think of the result of the painting or the outcome of the artist's life. Keep loving and becoming infatuated with art. Keep studying and drawing experience from everybody. But paint with our own fundamental qualities.

Youth is an effervescent and creative age. At this age, one must work as much as one can as one is at one's best.

January 5, 1976

Facing nature and man, one must dismiss all theories and must have a mutual sympathy with man and nature in one's painting.[1]

One ought to create a communion between paper, ink, pen, materials to produce one's work. Each material has its own tone which one must understand.

---

(1) *Cézanne once said: "Only nature, that's so fresh and beautiful, can be instructive to one's eyes. In order to be so, one has to train one's way of looking, and one has to work real hard".*

National character isn't a theory or a fixed opinion, it's created by the sentiment and life of each man, each nation.

The essence and character of each man appear on his work and might be churlish, pure, or feeble, vigorous...

One ought to use many types of materials and paint in various styles to develop one's faculties.

March 28, 1976

The main concern is one's right bearing in painting[1].

Technique is similar to the bicycle one's using. Paying too much attention to it, one'll become a mechanic. One must have one's personal vehicle. All techniques are simply means.

While painting one must rebuff all fixed ideas. Once one's mind is filled with fixed ideas, anything that is poured in, would simply spill.

---

(1) Painter Nguyễn Sáng once said: "While painting one must change and look for various forms, but the main thing consists of not losing one's direction". And both painters Nguyễn Gia Trí and Nguyễn Sáng once asked me: "Will you dare to go to the ultimate end?".

220

Each material has its own strong and weak points. One must know how to use them up.

With his creative mind, anything the artist touches with his hand would become art.

Keep going, keep working, and never think of any aim to reach. The fact of finding some ephemeral beauty would already constitute a tiring process for the artist.

When painting we're using something tangible to deal with something invisible. Being implicated in arguments or literary emotion is very dangerous.

One must see the figures in a much clearer manner. One must paint in such a manner as to permit the viewer to distinguish this one tree from the other.

The main thing resides in the artist 's eyes, as when he looks steadily at the figures, his strokes and his colours will be steady.

June, 15, 1976

Keep one's spirit clear and bright. Don't let it be dazzled by wealth and glory. The artist's spirit is a burning

221

fire that nurtures art and man.[1]

Each artist must have his own step, which must be a genuine one. One must live true-heartedly to permit one's life to develop. Trees with sweet-scented flowers and sweet fruits are trees that really grow, that really live a vigorous and joyful life, in an unconscious manner, since they were tiny ones until they bloom and bear fruits... What must come, will come, if you know how to live and work rightfully, if you dare to envisage big things, go deeply into them and reach your aim.

One must have an active resistance against all temptations of wealth and glory. Money is the thing that permits one to live and work favourably, but once one has had enough of it, one must try one's best to stand aloof from it.[2]

---

(1) In my opinion, 17 thousand-year-old lines and colour patches depicting bulls in the cave of Lascaux emanated from the painters' mind spirit, which was from the same mind spirit source of abstractionists of the New York school. Without the depth of mind spirit, all arts would turn out to be useless amusements. Human mind spirit is unique; it came into existence prior to languages and religions...

(2) Artist Nguyễn Sáng used to say to young painters: "Money is like salt which is used as a condiment. It must be used with reasonable amount to enhance the flavour of a dish, any excessive use of it would spoil our taste". And he also said: "As for the sake of art, I could collect every dime to survive, but if it is not for the art's sake, even if money were spread on my way I would step on it and walk".

Never compare one's work with the ones of other people. Keep going deeply into one's innate orientation, so as to discover one's personal beauty.

Very few people can live for the sake of the present time. People usually live either because of their past or because of their future. While performing his art, the artist is living for the sake of the present time, with the most proper signification of the word.[1]

Being an artist, one must live with poverty and in straightened circumstances. Creating means one has to pass beyond oneself, looking for the new. Imitating one's own self of yesterday is detrimental.

February 20, 1977

One must make researches and create with all one's presentiments. Not creating with eyes and hands. But one must act as a blindman, straining after and groping in the dark night, in search of beauty. Like a mother with child, One cannot oblige one's child to be a girl or a boy,

---

(1) O. Paz, a poet, said to the effect that: "Poetry is the present. The present is the only place where we can experience the eternity. The eternity is reduced to the dimension of present because Man can perceive only the present".

beautiful or unsightly. One must hope and rely on one's own self, on one's own good fortune and virtue, and on one's own substance to give birth to a good and beautiful child. The artist just cannot decide on everything. But the artist has, deep inside his heart, the confidence that he'll create beauty.

July 30, 1977

It's not suitable to impose accordingly to one's desire. Don't do anything inconsistent with nature.[1]

One must make use of one's deep-seated qualities to develop all one's creative strength. There exists no smart and clever painting, there are only paintings painted with one's will, without performing acrobatics.[2]

---

(1) *Zhuangzi said: "Don't take human to kill heaven; don't take the human intelligence to kill the Heaven's will... Be careful not to lose one's heavenly nature. That is to turn back to one's nature".*
Picasso said: "What's the use of disguises and artificialities in a work of art? What counts is what is spontaneous, impulsive. That is the truthful truth. What we impose upon ourselves does not emanate from ourselves". (Sebartes, 1946, page 145).
(2) *Picasso also said: "What forces our interest is Cezanne's anxiety - that's Cezanne's lesson; the torments of Van Gogh - that is the actual drama of the man. The rest is a sham". (Zervos, 1935). (All Picasso's words are translated by Dore Ashton).*

In art as well as in life, many people are familiar with living the life of a "prisoner", therefore, they don't feel sad, and don't worry about their loss of freedom.

When painting one must feel free and must be way above all the materials one's using.

Learning from others means striving to understand the mental conception that caused them to paint so. As for studying the figures, the colours,things we can see with our eyes, it means that we're imitating their outward appearance.

Modern painting means painting painted from nature and man. As for things we've thought out and considered as modern, they're actually out-of-date, as they had existed before.

Modus operandi, "Freely develop accordingly to one's capacity". Similar to trees and grass that grow, the trees might have a long, or a short life: The banana tree lasts a few months, the jack-tree five or ten years. It's the same thing with man, a fast development or a slow one depends on each individual.

When painting, one doesn't need any praise, and isn't afraid of any depreciation, as well as doesn't need to sell. One works in compliance with one's conscience and desire.

The whole thing comes from one's mind. One shouldn't distinguish decoration from painting.

November 26, 1977

One cannot convey one's sentiment to one's painting. "Good wine needs no bush". The painting will exactly convey all that one has in oneself.

Art means the creation of an equilibrium. Balance of sentiments.Balanced composition. Other common sentiments in ordinary life ought to be moderated.

Performing art is aimed at avoiding stupidity. Art means researches. Were one to know all the beauties, then it wouldn't be necessary to do research work or to paint any more.

June, 22, 1978

Sentiments are like petrol, when poured into a motor, it starts, but when poured over the ground, it's simply a kind of water. One must know how to manage, to harmonize one's sentiments.

The study of art must be a self-study. Each individual has his own presentiment. One must follow the guidance of one's presentiment. Theories are confined in a certain limit. As for presentiment, it breaks free from everything.

While studying one must know how to choose one's master and friends. One must know how to preserve one's presentiment. Never allow anyone to touch on one's presentiment. A master touching on the creative presentiment of his student is a poor master. [1]

In the choice of materials, whatever material is chosen, one must think of it all by oneself. One must adopt anything that's consonant with oneself, and mustn't listen to anybody. In our country, the oil often goes mouldy.

Abstract painting constitutes a new language, one can understand only upon working in it. It wouldn't be suitable if one decides to paint abstract painting in 10 years time. This matter might come while one is working. The artist works accordingly to his presentiment, not in accordance with theories. The more one works, the more one's presentiment turns prompt and effective. The question of heading towards great projects is like someone burning a fire, at first it's only a small fire, but later on, it becomes greater and greater.

---

(1) Poet Kahlil Gibran wrote about the teacher: "If he is indeed wise he does not bid you enter the house of his wisdom, but rather leads you to the threshold of your own mind".

The achieved paintings are unimportant. They are important only when one is working in them. Once achieved, they are like exercises that have been finished. One must head towards other things.

In days past, Manet [1] had looked for inspiration from Japanese painting, while Picasso [2] drew his inspiration from African statues. We can study and obtain something from each thing we look at, or we have seen.

Each artist has his own path, no one is similar to the other. Picasso, upon reproducing one of his own works, is also producing a fake Picasso [3].

The relation between the society and the artist is similar to the one between a tree and the ground, these two elements nourish each other.

Between the classic and the abstract paintings, the first genre uses its feet to walk, and the second one uses its head

---

(1) French painter (1832 – 1883)
(2) French painter of Spanish origin (1881- 1973)
(3) After saying so, painter Nguyễn Gia Trí related: A friend of Picasso told him that he possesses a painting by him. Picasso said: "It's a fake one". The friend was astonished: "I've seen you working on it with my own eyes, isn't it right?". Picasso answered: "It's a fake because I've reproduced it after one of my own paintings".

for the same purpose. One genre is a common language, the other one is a language which is newly developed.

With the common language, sometimes it isn't easy to understand each other, let alone speaking with the painting language.

With someone who studies painting at a higher degree, the teacher has turned into something that's troublesome. Try to choose the teacher one likes and try to select the paintings one feels pleasing to one's eyes.

November 26, 1978.

Art consists of looking for true things. Whatever one's individuality is, it'll appear exactly alike, without concealment, without forgery.[1]

Be always a student. Each achieved painting constitutes a means for one to study, to work. While working, think and look for ways to develop.

---

(1) Picasso once said: "It's not what the artist does that counts, but it's who and how he is that counts".
E.H. Gombrich one said: "There really is no such thing as Art. There are only artists".

Friends and teachers' help is only of secondary importance. The primary importance is one's own efforts. Like a tree that grows. From its growth, it tries to draw experience.

Question: Being a modern painter towards the end of the 20th century, if one happens not to know anything about Picasso's paintings, can one create something new?
Answer: There might be some painters of nowadays that have never heard about Picasso. Art is like flowers and fruits. They multiply themselves and grow everywhere. Their flavours might be fairly similar or different. If one adopts other peoples' patterns while painting, or imitates then one is only producing a fake work.

Viewing the painting, studying from other people's painting require a certain cultural standard, permitting one to understand, to perceive the matter.[1] While looking at many paintings, their influences might be sometimes good, sometimes bad. Pay attention not to be influenced by other people's features that aren't beautiful.

Generally speaking, one ought to work hard. After being sated with a material, one ought to shift to another one. One doesn't pursue art with one's intelligence.

---

(1) Painter Nguyễn Sáng related to me: While he was still an art school student (in the 40's of the last century), one day while he was looking at a Picasso's book of painting in a bookshop beside the lake of the Returned Sword, a well-known Vietnamese teacher from the Fine arts school came to meet him and gave him a most sincere advice: "Don't look at this guy's works, he's bluffing!".

230

May, 4, 1979.

In the days of Van Gogh[1], Gauguin[2], and Cezanne[3]... the painters directly imitated nature. Until Picasso's time and ever since, it was exactly the contrary. Formerly, the frame of the painting was a window, and inside it was nature. Today a painting is a painting. In days past, three-dimensional space was created on a horizontal plane, now it's only two-dimensional as it's much truer.

Realizing oneself is already a big progress[4]. But, after having realized oneself, one must try to go beyond oneself. One mustn't be influenced by that realization, to be able to free oneself. When learning to paint, one must think by oneself, must go by oneself. Keep having a thorough insight into one's own heart, and one will never go astray. An authentic artist never goes astray. As when an artist is making researches, the place he might go astray in is always interesting, wherever it might be. Even though he has gone astray into hell, he then has had a chance to see hell. This is because he's always researching in a fair-minded

---

(1) Dutch painter (1853 -1890).
(2) French painter (1848-1903).
(3) French painter (1839-1906).
(4) When I asked: "When does a painter see himself", he immediately answered: "One must be dead to be able to see oneself!". Then he said the above mentioned sentence.

and in a clear and bright way. The most dangerous learning is the one that follows suit other people, or that goes astray into wealth and glory.

Imitating nature is aimed at catching hold of the rules of nature. And from that situation, one tries to create something stronger than nature. In days past, people made wings, like a bird's wings, and were able to fly a short distance. But that was also an outer appearance, they didn't have any inner flying strength. Therefore, they were even inferior to a birdie. Also imitating the birds and nature, people have invented the aircraft and missiles. Such imitations constitute a quite different progress.

Each painting is a living body. It has its own life. It would effect on the viewers, were they to have the same emotions to share with it.

Question: In the course of studying and creating, should one paint with precision before proceeding with researches?
Answer: Stating the question like that is right, but one shouldn't be too stiff. The big changes must be decided by oneself, as one knows oneself best.

Concerning abstraction, Chinese characters constitute a kind of abstraction. Asians went directly into abstraction and were pioneers.

September 19, 1979

The artist's merit consists of cleansing the eyes of people at large. Thus permitting them to have a brighter, clearer, and newer look. To reach this aim, the artist must have a new look, a new mind. A too classical conception, as well as a too classical mind wouldn't be profitable for creation.

The artist uses his own modest rule and statute to grope and search for the great rule and statute.

With the lac-varnish, as well as with all other materials, one mustn't oblige it to conform with one's wish, while on the contrary one must have regard for the material, must understand it and follow its bent to manage.

On a board[1], a canvas[2], or on a sheet of paper, the artist is absolutely free ; if he happens not to have absolute freedom, then it's because he's binding himself with certain prejudice or rule.

Question: How should one use technique in one's creation?
Answer: Solving the question of technique means reaching perfection, and being satisfied with everything regarding one's painting.

---

(1) Wood body wrapped in fabric and coated with lac-varnish, used for painting a lacquer work.
(2) Canvas stretched over a wooden frame, used for oil paintings.

If still unsatisfied, one has to keep on searching and working.

An art work is similar to the moon. It shines upon rivers and lakes, as well as upon a cup of water.

Question: What is painting?
Answer: Painting is a plastic art. Its source is plasticity.[1] An abstract painting also belongs in plasticity. Diverse are its figures, a stroke, a comma also constitutes a figure. Colors and figures aren't necessarily attached to each other as with Impressionism.

Chinese characters are a kind of abstract painting. From a figure close to reality, it has been simplified to become a signal.

I've read the translation of a poem by Su Tung-P'o that reads: *"People don't want to draw grass, trees, or man, as all these concrete things bind the emotion"*. I've tried to look for the original copy to read, but I didn't find it.

Paintings showing local customs or landscapes prevent the artist from transmitting his emotion to viewers in others countries[2].

---

(1) Rodin said: "Beauty is something that has a figure".
(2) Painter Mondrian said: "Human beings only meet with one another in things that are general". French contemporary philosopher F. Jullien said: "The general is not something that's existing, it's the work of intelligence, and through intelligence works, one little by little finds the general(...) in the globalization, the general concept runs the risk of being replaced by the uniform one".

In art, it's not suitable to be deliberate. There exist two verses:

"*One deliberately plants flowers, flowers don't bloom,*
One unintentionally puts some willow-trees into the ground, *the willow –trees turn luxuriant*"[1].

Generally speaking, this means "buying a good personal[2] bicycle to go out".

The True, the Good and the Beautiful are One, without any beginning or end. Everything that has reached absoluteness, holds in itself all these elements.

October 8, 1979

Art is a limited means to look for the unlimited. Art contains everything. Whoever looking for something, will find it. The more one is fervent, the more one longs for knowledge, the more one's requirement is high, the higher one's knowledge will be.

While painting, that is to say creating, one is like a groping blindman. The moment one reviews one's work is

---

(1) These two verses are found in a work by Kim Dung, and have been repeated several times by the artist, at times with different words.
(2) Personal technique.

the moment one awakes. One then has to retire within one-self, and asks oneself: is it good enough?[1]. Painting isn't an objective, it's only a means to set out looking for wisdom. While researching, the objective is always ahead. On a higher level, the means and the ultimate end are one. The painting and the artist are one.

Dealing with art, the primary thing one has to avoid is to produce a "made up" painting.[2]

Finding one's way into art, one just cannot use only the mathematic way. One cannot reach one's end solely with mathematics. The East precedes the West because it proceeds straight ahead, through immediate perception.

The plastic art has to make use of thing's appearance

---

(1) Picasso once said: "In order to put on canvas the sudden apparitions which come to me, I don't know in advance what I am going to put on canvas anymore than I decide beforehand what colors I am going to use. While I am working I am not conscious of what I am putting on the canvas. Each time I undertake to paint a picture I have a sensation of leaping into space. I never know whether I shall fall on my feet. It is only later that I begin to estimate more exactly the effect of my work". (Zervos, 1932, page XV).

(2) Picasso once said: "To arrive at abstraction, it is always necessary to begin with a concrete reality... Art is a language of symbols" and: "Whatever is most abstract may perhaps be the summit of reality..." (Brassai, 1966, page 241). Painter Nguyễn Sáng said: "The more the painting is abstract, the more it's beautiful".

to mention the incorporeality. One's low feelings will call up a low graded art.

With the artist, rich or poor doesn't make sense.

From a concrete figure, raised to an abstract figure that might be fine, or coarse, depends greatly on the painter's nature.

One has to use one's mind as a merestone to travel onboard the "Bát Nhã" (Prajna, sanscrit word for wisdom) boat, when orientation is no longer available, or when the things' appearances one has used have been outpaced by oneself...

Each artist creates his own public. A man in a certain nature would like an art of the same nature.

The most correct study consists in avoiding to study from "the top". The paintings of world painters we are viewing are the tops, the flowers, among which some have fallen.

When one allows a change to occur as fast as a blink of an eye, then one doesn't have any decided view while working, that is to say while painting and creating.

Painting and creating can be compared with a brim-full

bowl of water, one retains all that remains and develops it.

April 29, 1980

Art is a means to elevate one's own individuality, bettering it more and more.

Question: In 1960, you went to Japan to buy lacquer materials. How did the Japanese paint lacquered paintings according to all what you've seen?
Answer: Nothing special.[1]

Question: Why Japan that has an ancient tradition of lacquer painting, and possesses highly artistic ancient lacquered works, doesn't use lacquer in its contemporary art at the present time?
Answer: May be because of prejudices.[2]

---

(1) In 1999, on the 50th China's nation founding anniversary, the Chinese Ministry of Culture threw a Chinese made lacquered paintings exhibition in Hồ Chí Minh city. Despite many painters participating in the exhibition, and there were so many paintings displayed but it seemed there was nothing special offered.
(2) Painter Nguyễn Gia Trí started to be passionately fond of lacquered paintings upon seeing painter Trần Quang Trân's lacquered works. Painter Trần Quang Trân himself had gone to Japan to study the Japanese traditional lacquer technique, which he brought back and applied to the contemporary lacquer painting in Vietnam. According to French researchers, since Vietnam was a poor country, her traditionnat lacquer techniques for daily use were so basic. In my opinion, the best traditional lacquer techniques were for decoration on Buddha statues or in temples, pagodas, or hallowed shrines.

238

Starting to paint lacquered paintings means one has already started to paint abstract ones. As it's not real as in ordinary daily life. The lacquerer looks into his innermost feelings, and doesn't look at the outer appearances of things.

The reason for which lacquer has leanings towards gold and vermilion, is that it's more inclined towards Yin, like colours in the space of communal houses, pagodas, temples and palaces.

The lacquerer paints quite a great deal as the more he paints, the more he "becomes addicted" to it. And each day he becomes even "more addicted". And concerning this matter, there exists no other material that might replace lacquer.

Painting is a type of special activity, different from all other ones, it's not right to say that one must be rich before starting to paint.

Lacquered paintings require a peculiar technique. While painting lacquered works, one cannot look with habits similar to the ones applied to oil painting.

Vietnamese lacquerware is a brand new technique. It has its own method for settling the question and for painting.

One shouldn't use a material to rough another material out. Painting too many silk paintings will create bad working habits. While studying and working, were one to be "too clever", one will progress slowly.

The painter doesn't work to illustrate any philosopher.

While producing, the artist has his own thoughts. He shouldn't care about explaining or analysing like writers or critics.

A painter who fails to understand and who cannot paint in oil, will not be able to understand and to paint lacquered paintings.

August 1, 1980

I've committed many mistakes while working, and that's the reason why I'm making great progress. Were I to paint too cleverly, I would develop slowly.

If there were no Mr.I[1] and assistant Thành, there would be no lacquered paintings produced by myself.

Great is Mr. I's public virtue.[2]

See note on page 37.

240

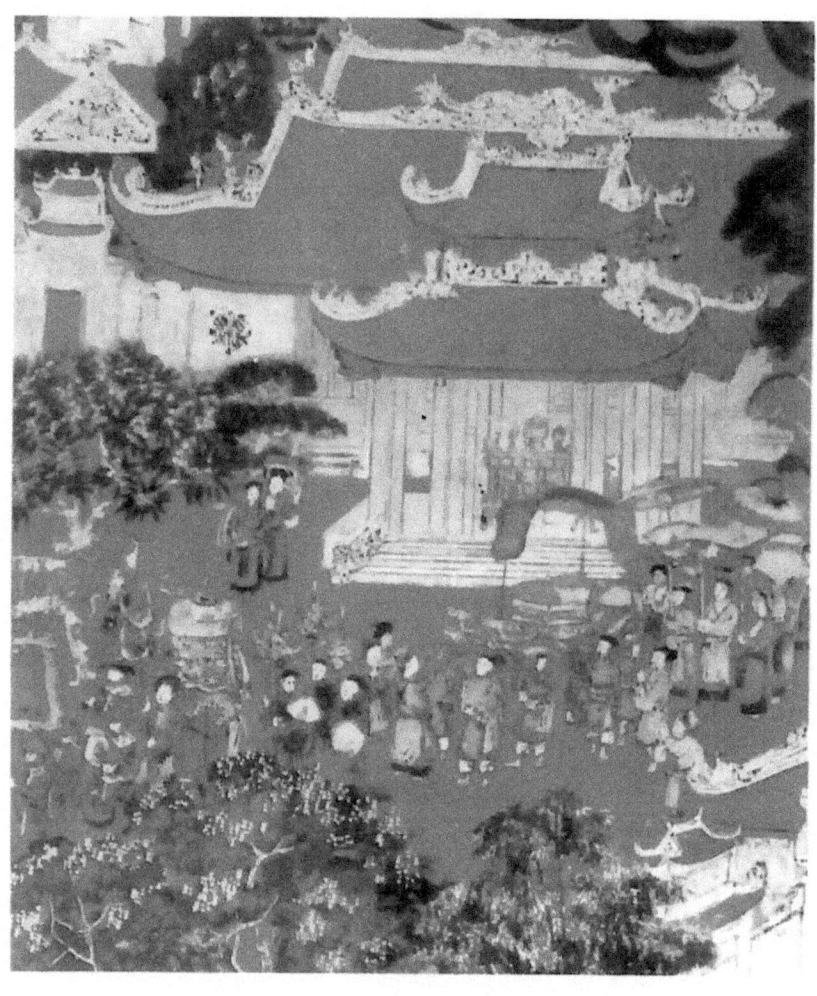

- Tranh "*Lễ rước thần ở Đền Đô*" (Đình Bảng nơi thờ 8 vị vua triều nhà Lý) - 1969
(Trích đoạn) sơn mài của họa sĩ Nguyễn Gia Trí
- Geniuses' greeting festival procession extract from a lacquer by artist Nguyễn Gia Trí

In the past, upon seeing me working in lacquers, Mr.I, who was an oil painter, just couldn't understand the question of "time" in lacquer painting. He liked lacquer very much and quite wanted to try painting it, but each time he saw and met with lacquer, it immediately "ate"[3] him, so he had to give up.

---

(1) Painter Joseph Inguimberty, familiarly called Mr. I, by assistant Thanh (craftsman and lacquerer) and the students of the Indochina school of Fine Arts, is very whole-hearted vis-à-vis his students; he gave examples by means of painting many times in the field, and elaborately studying the nature in Vietnam with oil paint. He directed his students into the lives of professional painters. Painter Nguyễn Gia Trí relates: "Mr. I introduced people who ordered paintings from me, sometimes there were so many clients that I chose the ones I like. One day he brought to me a client that I didn't want to serve, so he asked me: "Do you intend to choose also the personality of the orderer?" The painters from the Indochina school of Fine Arts recounted: Painter J. Inguimberty rectified and asked the students to repaint each one of the bent stroke of the temple roof. When the war spread to Hanoi, the School allowed the students to evacuate, while no more colours were sent from France, Mr. I.organized the hand-crushing of oil paint to provide the school with colours...

(2) According to painter Quang Phòng: "In the development of lacquer painting, Mr. Joseph Inguimberty has quite a great deal of merit. He has made throughout researches on "the lacquer of Annam" and was as well-experienced as Mr. Phó Thành (i.e. craftsman Đinh Văn Thành 1898-1977), the man he's so close with throughout his 20 years of teaching in Hanoi. Being a principal teacher of oil painting, he had neglected his mission, as he was so infatuated with lacquer and continually watched for the students' lacquer works to guide them and to provide them with the most effective solutions in the realization..."

(3) To be allergic to lacquer and to get swollen face, hand, foot...

With each lacquered painting, one proposes to oneself a lesson with problems to solve: stroke, shifting limit of the stroke, change of background colours, black over vermilion, red over black, black over silver etc...

Painting is close to religion as it originates from people's innermost feelings. It isn't made by brain or hand.

One has to work much. One must train to boss lacquer. Pay attention to dark and light changes of small details on the painting.

Each artist is a separate world, which no one can throughly understand.

November 19, 1980

While performing art, the most essential thing consists of being completely true-hearted.The most harmful things is being artificial vis-à-vis oneself. One has to work seriously, and at times, must even be rough on oneself. Producing hundreds of spoiled ones, to obtain only one good one, or even a half of a good one. The artist must never be self – satisfied.

The materials occupy one half of the artist. He must love the materials as much as he loves his wife, so as to have a child, that is to say his produced work. Each

242

material has its own characteristic. The artist has to apprehend its particularity. For example: the degree of thickness or thinness of oil paint. With lacquers, it's question of the smoothness of the surface, the degree of brightness, or whatever requirements, provided that artistic results are obtained. Whenever an expectation remains unfulfilled, the painter feels uneasy, looking for ways to make good, until he's partly or fully satisfied with his work.

Between the rough and the work is a continuous process. The rough is only a careful preparation for the work itself. Besides, one must ponder over the way to achieve it with good result. Painting is a method of Zen.

Someone has quoted: "He has mixed his emotional soul with his painting". They are considering the soul as something thickish that could be ground and mixed with colours, then used for smearing the surface of the painting!

That's just because the artist wants to know and see his soul, that he makes researches and try to work. He paints because he doesn't know.

With regard to abstractionism, one shouldn't distinguish it from other schools. It's only a means for the artist to look for the truth. Abstract painting is difficult because the artist cannot lean on true models. Each point, each stroke in an abstract painting has its own figure that is a part of the painting's oneness. Details are like dew-drops. But, each one of them is illuminated by the sunlight. All details on the painting must be subject to a similar control.

When Pollock[1] paints an abstract painting, he "enters into a trance" and amalgamates himself with the painting,considering himself as "one" with it, that is to say as a part of the painting itself. All emotions in life reveal themselves.[2]

Learning to paint is like someone learning to ride a bicycle, at first, one feels staggering, swaying, then one, later on, succeeds to recover the equilibrium, and can pedal straight ahead.

Painting means working all by oneself,discovering and drawing experience all by oneself. Painting wriggling lines isn't enough. As each stroke, each figure must be thought of thoroughly to obtain good result, seeming like "unmindful", and natural as a breath.

Japanese paintings, that seem quite simple, actually require much great pains to achieve. This can be compared

---

(1) Jackson Pollock, American painter (1912-1956).
(2) Once artist Nguyễn Sáng told me: "There should be plastic arts for the universe". That was an all-embracing and important statement in modern painting. For example, with pure and abstract painting, Pollock has opened the universal forms of his mind.

with someone who doesn't know how to drink tea accordingly to the "Tea Cult" of the Japanese, and who thinks the tea is weak. Such weakness is also the result of a lot of training.

Failure as well as success have an equal value. As both situations serve for urging the artist to head forward.[1]

When reading, it suitable to read the author's original text, as one shouldn't read the mediatory works. Learning to pain, one should avoid reading articles on painting by art critics.

While producing, at times, one might be like in a dream. The painter worked but didn't think. As when one thinks, one is painting an abstract work, the work realized is no longer abstract. At such a moment, the act of producing has been divided into two parts, and lies between the painter and the painting itself.

All remains natural. Upon painting to depict a certain idea, one has produced an illustration. At higher levels, one knows how to pay attention to the composition, style etc ...

---

(1) Picasso once said: "We must always look for perfection. Obviously, for us, this word no longer has the same meaning. To me, it means: from one canvas to the next, always go further, further..." (Brassaï, 1966, page 85).

Facing nature, one can still draw from it an abstraction. At times, through a concrete appearance, one can perceive some abstraction.

Painting is like eating. One has to eat many dishes to become a gourmet, and to know how to cook. Upon achieving a painting, one has to think of it and draw experience: the intentional fulfilments, the good results, the failures ....

In days past, my master often prompted me: " Beware of habits, or of a matter of knack". A good knack is acceptable. A bad knack, in the long run, will become dangerous, incurable. Formerly, my master had put his heart and soul into teaching me. Now I'm doing the same thing to you.

When the Japanese occupied Indochina, the Allied aircraft bombed Hanoi. As my master and I sat deep inside a shelter, Mr. I told me: *"In a wartime like this, I'm obliged to give up My Great Dream"*.

February 2, 1981

An authentic artist constantly turns to the source. The fertile and endless creative inspiration originates from the source. If a tree is luxuriant and has many flowers and fruits, it's thanks to its roots. At that source, art and religion meet with each other.

246

One's mind is something very immature, that could easily be dwarfed or stone-dead.

Painting means knowing by heart, having something in one's heart. When painting one immediately catches hold of the thing one sees.

With a masterpiece, although a small fragment is cut wherever from it, this fragment still has the breath of life of the whole work, as well as blood and flesh.

The reason why the "Nan-Houajing" of Zhuangzi is mild and flexible, is that because it's alive. Only a dead master is "solid", "firm", "stony"[1].

---

(1) *The first time I read the Nan-Houajing" translated by Nhượng Tống (famous Vietnamese translator), I was passionately fond of it, and it seemed like I had gone astray into a new and strange world. Later on, I met with a series of works by Nietzsche such as: "Schopenhauer, the educator", "The Twilight of Gods", "Thus, spake Zarathoustra..." and I once again met with another world, red-hot, vigorous, inspiring. I suddenly found the Nan-Houajing tasteless, weak and supple. Upon exchanging views with the master, he has had the above mentioned remark. He also had his own remark: Nietzsche's thinking originates from somewhere in India. And he had spoken about Nietzsche two or three times, scatteringly: "He's mad". Although in the later part of his life, Nietzsche became insane with me Nietzsche remains a great thinker of mankind as he once dealt with the importance of thought: A thinker is more important than all universities and all nations...*

When painting with whatever material, one becomes "the incarnation" of it. One must work in a long time with a unique material to perceive the progress.

Like a pilot or an astronaut who trains for the ability to put up with the lack of oxygen, by means of pressing buttons for emergency aid gas. While performing art, whenever being blocked at some spot, one has to convert. Convert while constantly maintaining one's creative inspiration. Always remember: creative inspiration doesn't depend on things.

Lacquered painting requires an absolutely smooth surface. Even if there is only a tiny scratch, while rubbing carbon powder, one must rub anew.

The transferring of drawings, drawn on paper, to lacquer material is like someone that has a target in the east, but shoots in the west. Compared with materials, it's like an architectural chart.

Whether the painting is finished[1] or not, depends on oneself. The main problem consist of knowing what one needs from that painting? One ought to know what one does want?

---

(1) Completely achieved.

248

On each painting, one strives to realize a certain desire, and one has to constantly test the capacity of materials. One should realize on each painting certain emotional or aesthetic effect.[1]

Art is something that cannot be spoken about. Therefore all researchers and critics' arguments are fallacious.

The developments of the mind is similar to the ones of chemical products, that are quite complicated and difficult to deal with. Books are precious because they give rise to matters we have had in our mind, making them clearer.

Each material is like some food to chew. Chewing until exhausted,then shift to another one.

With regard to each change in emotion and creation, one must listen attentively to one's mind directives, and adopt them. This is something no one can tell us.

The artist lives with the whole universe, East, West, ancient as well as modern. Creating means living out of the current time. The artist lives with the gaur paintings in grottoes, with Leonardo da Vinci etc... Living in an artistic way

---

(1) Picasso once said: "I want to get to the stage where nobody can tell how a picture of mine is done. What's the point of that? Simply that I want nothing but emotion given off by it". (De Zayas, 1923).

is very difficult. Some have become as mad as a March hare like Van Gogh, or turned addicts like Utrillo, Modigliani...

One has to know the figures by heart to be able to paint quickly, accurately.

In my second academic year, I could no longer abide the school and had to give up.[1] Later on, as the lacquered painting department was founded, I returned to it. The academy-figure hour in the morning was for me a torture, I had eagerly waited for the afternoon to work in lacquered painting.

Figures are steady thanks to the relations in the composition, as a whole, but not because of any part.

Painting lacquers is like painting in the Middle Age. This is because it requires a great length of time.

---

(1) His little brother, Architect Nguyễn Gia Đức related: "When my brother quit the Fine Arts School, Master V. Tardieu came to see me and advised: "Try to look for your brother and ask him to resume his studies, it would be a waste were he to give up". The French teachers are people who love beautifulness, therefore they particularly appreciate the talented students. According to artist-painter Quang Phòng: "With us, the greatest merit of Master Victor Tardieu is that he had foreseen and strived his best to safeguard the national character for the Vietnamese students by means of encouraging them to return to the source and to be close to their time".

Nature, from the butterfly's wings, or the cockroach, is always beautiful. As for what I'm producing myself, though toilsome, bitter, is always unsightly.

February 26, 1981

I dare not write any criticism. Otherwise, I wouldn't be myself. The main thing is whether the painter feels that his work is "alluring" or not? As when painting, one paints for oneself, not for sale, or for displaying sake. One has to ask oneself everything.

The painting is the "means", like "the finger which points at the moon"[1] of Buddha. Lot of people don't see the moon, but they keep on showing, and they show at sixes and ill-sevens.

One has to change one's means to have a "constantly new mind".

In front of a wood panel one is preparing to paint, one has to retire within oneself and "move away all rubbish" (reminiscences of paintings painted by other people and complicated sentiments) before starting to paint.

------

(1) Buddha shows the difference between the means and the end in the "Thủ Lăng Nghiêm" (Sùrangama-sama2dhi-Sutra canonical book).

Art begins only when one turns "non-ego".[1] It's not Nguyễn Gia Trí, Trần Văn Cẩn, Nguyễn Xuân Việt etc..., but it's lacquer living its own life. Like vegetation in nature, it adapts itself and develops accordingly to its natural condition, and cannot be coerced. Everything must be in an orderly fashion. One cannot be in a hurry. One cannot go right through without stopping.

Question: Does abstract painting destroy or weaken the real figures?

Answer: Is one afraid that abstract painting would influence real figures? There will be a certain influence. But, just like dishes, once eaten, digestion will follow, but one cannot see directly how the digestive system works

In days of yore, Hokusai painted a painting, used his wooden shoes to tread on it, spat on it, and it became an art work all the same. Endowed with a painting "vital fluid", one can keep colours in one's mouth and spit on the painting to obtain a sun all the same. It's not because of one's dexterity.

---

(1) Scholar Nguyễn Duy Cần wrote: "Since it is "non-technical", "non-attempting", "unnamed", then they and the Way are one. "The Way does not work, and there is nothing that doesn't work. Therefore their action is not directed by evil desires, but rather by the Way, the Reality and the Non-ego".

As for societies, a western philosopher has written, "The more civilized the society is, the more non-self it becomes".

The "finger which points at the moon" represents the means. Without it, at times, one can even use a broom.

"One deliberately plants flowers, flowers don't bloom,
One unintentionally puts some willow - trees into the
ground, the willow-trees turn luxuriant"

Someone had drawn a cartoon: one plants a young tree, then places next to it a stick, planted on the ground, to let it lean on, and as a result, the tree withered while the stick was in bloom, painting is exactly alike.

Question: Confucianism claims that "man" is at its source. Thus, is it true that the source of the artist is also "man"?
Answer: Right. As the painter is also a man, but not a man in flesh and blood.

Question: What is the difference between Eastern and Western philosophies?
Answer: Like rice and bread[1]

Painting abstract is like conquering the moon. One has to make ready one's can of oxygen, as it's different up there. And then, the earth and stone up there is always the same earth and stone, as the ones down here.

_____._____

(1) He once related: "In my younger days, I enjoyed reading philosopher H.Bergson very much".

Practicing from small paintings, just like practicing neat- and-square penmanship, so that later on, one can write the big characters. And one must also know how to rely on oneself.

July 10, 1981

In days past, I painted abstract paintings, I tore paper into pieces and shook them on the board to see the change. Just like soothsayers that looked at the changes of the cards, then used their personal connection with the metaphysical world to judge.

Question: Only Buddha can use his finger to point at the moon. What happens when one isn't Buddha?
Answer: That's only an example, one can take another example such as: Art is a means for us to go into a world we've never known before.

Each work is a left-behind means. As ordinary people often cannot create the means, so they have to buy them for their own use.

The misapprehension of means and ends leads to harmful errors.

Upon producing, one is like an acrobat that performs on the flying trapeze and swings up and down, then, at a certain span, has to drop his arms.[1] At first, he has to practice with a safety net. Once exerced, he doesn't need the safety net anymore.

When painting a lacquered work, one can at first prepare on paper. Upon starting to work in the lacquer, one uses lacquer paint. Just like one cannot translate all the beauties of a poem from one language into another one, we don't "translate" the painting on paper into a lacquered one. This is because each material has its own characteristic and life.

Producing is like delivering. Without yearning, one cannot produce any work.

Going deeply into a branch, one can understand other branches. Philosophy is the source, from which one can understand other things. Reading canonical books is very difficult, one has to have a good guide to be able to understand.

One has to thoroughly understand the substance of lacquer paint to get a chance to manage it.

---

(1) Painter Nguyễn Sáng once said: "Upon working on a painting, one doesn't know when... it's finished". As for Picasso, he had said several times that: When an artist decides to finish a painting, he's killing it at the same time, "Unfinished, a picture remains alive, dangerous. A finished work is a dead work, killed". (Haesaerts, 1961, page 7).

September 26, 1981

A lacquered painting can be preserved for a long time, as long as possible, and the longer the better. While polishing and shining, the gold and silver remain intact.

Lacquer also has its own life: also young, old, and dead[1]. Upon painting a lacquered work, one must realize that lacquer has its own reason.

Upon producing, one is at times dreaming, at times awakened, and at times fainting... No one reproduces a dream.

The intention concerning a lacquer develops in an unforeseen manner. Whatever might happen, the lacquerer has to maintain his initial intention. Like a man's life, there are many things that cannot be decided previously. The painting itself doesn't have any intention.

Painting a lacquered work is difficult, so one has to train to familiarize oneself with difficult things. The artist mustn't be easygoing, so the more he meets with difficulties the better. It's a means for him to test his will.

---

(1) He said this to explain that one must leave a long time for the paint on the wood body to stop shrinking, the surface will become smooth, and its fibres and canvas grain will disappear.

256

Just like wading in the mud and climbing up a mountain, all other materials, when compared with lacquer, are also like that. One must go through painful experiences to know how to rightly appreciate happiness. One must know what is unsightly to know what is beautiful.

On abstract paintings, one must know how to choose beautiful spots to develop. Just like a cook must know the flavours of the dishes he's cooking.

The painting doesn't only have two dimensions, as it still has a profundity, the painter's profundity.

In my schooldays, there was one time when I made a rough of a lacquer and failed continually. Each day, Mr.I came into the classroom, looked at my lesson and shook his head (while teaching, Mr.I rarely speaks and usually "nods" his head and "shakes" it, and points at the acceptable or unacceptable spot on the painting). After one week in which I had done my lesson, Mr.I asked me: "*Are you painting a landscape at Hòn Gai?*" (a place where coal is exploited) as the sky is black and the ground is also black. At that time, It was like the Zen Buddhists that used to say "Ngộ" (be enlightened), I asked myself: "*How come the tiles are red, the walls white, while the sky is black and the earth also black?*". And I suddenly understood: Lacquer has its particular "justification". Lacquer is completely different from oil paint.

Painting materials are substances the artist has to transform into art, into his own soul.

One has to work in lacquer to understand the "matière"[1]. Formerly, I had thought that "matière" means when one draws an apple, it must have the substance of a real apple. Substance isn't the substance of the object. Producing with all other materials is also good, if one considers it as an exercise.

People that are well up in techniques often have very little creative mind. As the creative mind is something weak and immature. When it thickens or hardens, it will become dry and stiff and dead[2].

Generally speaking, in art and literature, painting usually takes precedence over other things. For example: the artisrt first created the tunic, then people write proses and poems, or compose songs about it[3]...

Practice to distinguished black tones, vermilion tones. Each painting is an exercise. One must know how to love and to be passionately fond of difficulties while producing. Loving only the achieved work isn't correct.

See note on page 55.

One can work in several lacquers at a same time. This matter depends on each one of the painters, it might be easy with some of them, and difficult with some others. Just like with jugglers, they can turn 10 plates at the same time on tops of sticks.

Each one of my paintings is only an exercise I've given to myself. Speaking out like that, may be the buyers will not buy anymore.

People that buy paintings, often and mostly buy only a signature that has become well-known.

---

(1) French word for substance of the painting.

(2) One time, I showed him a lacquered painting of mine that is fairly beautiful but not profound. He took me to the garden   and pointed at a newly bloomed orchid bulb that had the same beauty: unattractive, without scent. He kept silent and pointed at the heads of the bunches of green orchid roots. He once pointed at a beautiful detail on the work entitled "Centre-South-North Spring Garden" and said: "retain the new" and at a place that isn't beautiful enough, he told me: "One must know how to endure the unsightly".

(3) In the Renaissance in Italy, Michelangelo (1475-1564), painter, poet, architect, and famous sculptor had said: "..he who thinks well and understands clearly the human works will see at once that all Man's achievements are nothing more than painting, or a part of painting".

Today, E.Powell (Conservator of the American National Museum) also perceives that: "the expressive elements and the artistic means have caused art to become the centre of human experience".

Everything contained in the work, is known only to its author.

October 9, 1981

Each thing has its respective justification.

The surface, the summit of art, like nature, has thousands of types. So the essential is to perceive the inner "justification".

To use eggshells, one must have a creative mind, if used only to replace the white colour, then there's nothing special.

While producing, one has previous intentions, but there exist natural beauties that appear, which one must know how to retain them.

December 11, 1981

Lacquered and oil paintings are two quite different worlds. One cannot take the plastic beauties of lacquered paintings, and use them for oil paintings. One cannot patch and it cannot be patched. It has to be a whole slab. It must be itself, unmixed.

Fast or slow doesn't make sense, as time is in one's own heart. One can paint up, or down, or in whatever direction. As painting is like one's own handwriting. When one identifies oneself with one's work, it becomes oneself, and one oneself turns into it. In such a moment, one is able to distinguish even the tiniest mistake, just like the conductor of a symphonic orchestra that can distinguish the smallest note that gets out of tune.

With a painting, one has to leave out all intentions. This is because whenever one wishes to do something intentionally, there's already a distance between oneself and the materials. While one's effort to realize one's intention creates an even bigger distance.

It's always so when one identifies oneself with the whole work, and it's not because when one pays attention to small details that one can achieve success. One must always look at the wholeness, at the big thing.

Only by painting lacquered paintings, can one understand time and life. Lacquer is a means for one to live and it's also the end. At a certain moment, these two elements will blend.[1]

_____

(1) Master Thuận Thiện preached his sermon: "The Way and Life are like the two wings of a bird, without one the bird would not be able to fly".

Anything that is a means, cannot be the end.[1]

Live righteously, sufficiently, and then when one dies, one will see that one has lived properly, sufficiently, and has not wasted one's life, so finally, one can die a serene death.

Life and death are like black and white colours. These two elements appear intermittently, intermingle with each other, just like dark and light shades on a painting, and blend.

It's not suitable to say: "*It's a real pity to compare the artist's happiness with that of the ordinary people*". Saying so, one is offending through haughtiness. As we cannot know how people feel in their inner heart. The best thing to do is to live a simple life. As the more one is haughty, the more one day one will drop down to the bottom.

I'm not painting anything. Other people paint, and the material paints itself.

Throughout my life, I've been working in lacquered paintings. I only want to demonstrate their utility vis-à-vis

---

(1) *His speech as well as his painting always heads towards something marvelous, difficult to seize, and at times seemingly contradictionary. He once spoke vaguely: "From haziness, clearness is brought forth".*

the plastic arts. As, although meeting with precious materials, people have left them aside, laughed at them and despised them.[1]

One depends much on materials and means. Lacquer materials are beautiful and contain many fortuitous factors. But the difficulty resides in oneself, not in the things. One is hard to please, and the fact of being dissatisfied with what one has realized,obliges one to meet with other more difficult problems.

---

(1) The sentence: "Proving that the lacquer paint is a material used for painting" seems quite simple but upon comparing with Japan and China, with their huge traditional painting heritage, then we can see that they also couldn't create anything brilliant and original for modern world painting and then we can conceive that to so high a degree painter Nguyễn Gia Trí's work is so hard and difficult. Proving that lacquer paint is a material used for painting means sharing one half of the modern world with oil paint, and thus continuing to maintain the creative fire of world painting: "The Paris school" and "The New York school"... The remark of S.S. Averintsev (Member of the Institute of Sciences in the former USSR) will show us the preciosity of painting:

"The most convincing art basic is: "The place in which aesthetics exists is also the place where God is present amidst the people, as aesthetics proves God's presence". And "beauty isn't "purely" the beauty, but it's also a criterion of Truth, and moreover, it's the deepest and most basic criterion of truth".

Phan Bội Châu, a revolutionary, a great thinker of Việt Nam, in his interpretation of the Y-King has written: "Once we have the way, everybody will be with us".

Concerning the composition and the question of painting on all four sides, one cannot decide everything all by oneself.

Whenever there's a scratch on the painting, hold it lightly inclined and look at all four sides, and one will see all the scratches. Upon being shone, the scratch will appear even clearer.

I can paint forever.

Go ahead and paint, one doesn't need to know what figure it is, it will be rectified later.

February 5, 1982

Painting is like riding on a bicycle, one ought to ride moderately fast, or fairly fast to be able to maintain equilibrium and prevent oneself from falling.

Working in a lacquered painting is difficult as one has to keep one's initial intention throughout a long time. Some of my paintings took up to seven years. In that process, there were many changes that occurred in my mind. Therefore, one has to know how to greet them, then one must see what should be retained, as well as what should be given up.

Working in lacquers, the artist has to enter into a

difficult world, which none of the materials has ever met with. Like someone learning to jump high up that binds a sandbag at his foot, from a light to a heavier weight. Once the sandbag has been taken off, the heavier it was, the higher one can jump.

Upon producing with eggshells as well with water colours, one doesn't need to pay attention to figures. But one must constantly pay attention to materials, to the whole amounts of colours, so as to cause eggshells and lacquer paint to blend into a unique slab.

Don't pay attention to the surrounding perimeter of the drawing[1], but pay attention to the whole area. Observing the drawing on the tracing paper, the figures are lenghthened.

Pay attention to the connecting clefts of eggshells. The eggshells, although flat polished, still have furrows. If one applies silvery and red – brown paint (called cánh gián in Vietnamese as it resembles the colour of the cockroach wing) then the furrows still appear.[2]

---

(1) Figures.
(2) When teaching, he also taught shrewdness, as well as the most meticulous behaviour just like one is in an atmosphere in which Liệt Tử's work is related. He once said: "A fly that alights on the wood body would make it subside". When I asked him: "When gluing silver, what must one do to make the edges conterminous?". He answered: "Keep rubbing slowly and vigorously until your thumb is cut", while the silver leaf used in lacquerware is laminated at the thinnest extent.

In one's relations with everything, one is always using things, and cannot be used by things.

Upon preparing the rough, one has to figure out of the way to proceed with. Figure out and foresee a certain number of contingencies.

Everything that turns professional is considered as a failure.

June I, 1982

A scholar must be at the same time a philosopher to have a great vision of the problem, otherwise,he's only an ordinary mathematician.[1]

Seizing quickly the slightest idea that occurs in one's mind. A painting, as a whole, has to be painted at one stretch. All details must appear at the same time on whatever spot. If the face is drawn in one hour, while the hand takes only fives minutes, then it's a lack of consistency.

---

(1) Artist Nguyễn Sáng says: "Every artist should be a thinker; his work would be great then". He also says: "The Earth which billion of people are living on is in fact like a grain of dust in the universe". A Russian scholar has also had this perception like that of a philosopher: Man can fly into the universe; if he has not made himself a clean one, he will only cause the turbidity of the universe.

Terminating a lacquered painting is like a last blink. Like Mozart listening to a whole piece of music in a blink, it must be the same thing with a painter.[1]

To train oneself, one has to learn to paint real quick.

Pollock's Action Painting: A long trail of paint dropping vertically, another trail of paint splashing horizontally. The dust of paint forms tiny dots on the painting; if looking through a magnifying-glass, one can see life bustling about in them.

Oil painting can easily turns the painter into a shallow-headed individual. Painting lacquer, one can train one's steadfastness to live together with the painting.

If one specializes oneself in making drawing, and rough sketch,then one isn't doing anything good, as the materials involved only reach that limit. The greater the scope of materials used, the more the work becomes difficult.

---

(1) A. Liberman: "It is said that Mozart could visualize his music as though it were a painting, could see the whole in one moment of time while other composers conceived their work within the passage of time". Concerning Cézanne way of painting. "So he used the harmonic principles of music, trying to establish for the art of painting the structural security and solidity that is particular to music". Descartes once said: "Everything is senseless if we fail to live with all our heart. Everything is senseless if we remain separated from philosophy".

On a lacquered painting or on an oil painting, a hesitating stroke or a high –falutin stroke can be seen easily.

"Enlighten oneself in order to enlighten others". One has to understand more profoundly. One's self is only a very tiny dot, enlighten oneself is very difficult, as for enlightening others, it's something immensely great.

Read directly the Buddhist Canonical Books, pay little attention to the base of Hinduism. Knowing about it's substance is already quite difficult.

Limit one's reading, as reading too much may lead to talking nonsense. Reading too much is harmful. Reading is like drinking wine to stimulate creation.

None of the paintings is considered as completed. All are rough sketches.[1]

Producing lacquers is as busy as nursing an infant.

---

(1) He's never satisfied with any of his works. I once asked him: "Do you want to look again at your paintings that are still conserved in our city?". He answered: "No, I don't want to look at old ones, as they cannot be repaired". Terminating the painting "Centre–South – North - Spring Garden" sizes 2m x 5.4m, at 82, he still wanted to create "Matière" spreading over the whole frame with designs of the painting, so as to make it fuzzy, thus decreasing the decorative nature and increasing the artistic nature. Due to his declining health, he had to leave it the way it is now.

Spending one's whole life to produce lacquers is as hard and humiliating as serving a life sentence.[1] Thus a "chain" might be transformed into a "necklace"... It would be difficult for one to gratuitously giving you some gold.

The way of living, taught by Buddhism, simply requires that, whatever one does must be "useful for oneself, as well as for other people".

June 21, 1982

Painting lacquer is not only to look with one's eyes and see beauty, but also to touch and perceive that it's smooth. It suits one's heart, as one has to be sincere with one's heart. Being sincere with oneself doesn't mean painting only in a honest way. The truth is much more complicated.

When proposing to oneself an aim to reach, one has to materialize it at any price. Whenever one has to break the law, then it's something beyond one's control.

Life is but a dream. When one sleeps, it's a dream.

---

(1) During the time he had to produce many works, he woke up at 3AM, drank tea, read a few pages, then prepared the pieces of work for his workmen (When there were many orders, his workshop had up to five workmen). In the evening, he used to correct the paintings, realized by his workmen, until 10-11 PM then went to bed.

It's also a dream when one is awake.[1]

Bolted gold spoils the preciosity of gold.

While creating, one is led by an invisible law.

One cannot coerce lacquer. Sometimes one has to please the painting just like one is pleasing one's mother.

In the painting process, one has to depend on the painting to make necessary changes, and must also follow close on the changes of the painting.

Laws concerning lacquer fixed by oneself: smooth, shiny, silvery, golden etc... provided that it's beautiful.

October 25, 1982

Asian painting shows certain mortification as it goes inwardly. European painting goes outwardly. The painting itself personifies the artist.

The law of causation is a great law. Like cause like effect. Speaking about cause and effect, one has included time in that law.

---

(1) Li Po has a famous verse: "Life is like a great dream. Let's take it easy we should'n work too hard".

Art knows no-want. As it knows no-want, it's ascending towards something extremely high.

Working in lacquer, it isn't good enough when one just sees with one's eyes and finds the work acceptable, actually, one's heart must also see it and give it's consent.

The main point is to train to acquire a pure and clean heart. As one doesn't need anything, one isn't impeded, and one heart is pure and clean.

Bookish knowledge, or knowledge brought by other people, isn't genuine knowledge.

Stop at the unknown. The unknown is another knowledge.

One knows without having to learn. Knowledge exists in one's inner self. When being born,no one learns to eat, drink, walk and live, but then everyone knows about all that.

Painting while feeling that one isn't painting at all, is also a good thing.

One can find one's own Nirvana. At times, people think that they are living in Nirvana, while they are actually in Hell.

Philosophy is involved in everything, from eating, drinking, walking, standing...

Lacquer has its own laws with regard to all aspects, one cannot impose on it the particular views of other materials.

Painting abstract works is very difficult, as abstract is quite bountiful.

While painting, don't get entangled in anything concrete. Leonardo has said: "One can paint better while looking at mossy walls".

At times, one can let other people look at one's work, and thanks to them, one will discover a few mistakes. As, by dint of looking at one's work oneself, one get used to it, and thus cannot see the mistakes.

With one's friends, sometimes their knowledge in other fields might help one to paint a better work, with more creativity in one's plastic art. As a painter doesn't only paint.[1]

Reading too much might cause one to go astray.

The main thing consists of not allowing oneself to

_____

See note on page 69.

272

Duy Thức Nhị Thập Luận (Vijñaptimātratāsiddhi ;
Viṃśatikā)
by Vasubandhu - Asaṅga
vô trước thế thân
Chinese version by Huan Chang Huyền Trang

Diệu Pháp Liên Hoa Kinh (Saddharma Puṇḍarīka Sūtra)
Kumārajīva' Chinese version of
Kinh Kim Cương the Vajracchedikā Sūtra .

go astray, to regress, while on the contrary one must discerningly develop oneself.

While producing one can break up small laws, but has to observe the big ones.

While working, cleverness constitutes an important factor. Cleverness can cover up the poorness of art. Cleverness is also something that serves genuine beauty. These are directions for use. One cannot realize a good work by means of being only unfeigned. To reach beauty, one has to make use of all one's abilities, among which figures cleverness

November 25, 1982

The main thing in life consists of preserving one's true intention.

---

(1) Picasso one said: "What do you thinhk an artist is? An imbecile who only has eyes if he's a painter, ears if he's a musician, or a lyre in every chamber of his heart if he's a poet, or even, if he's a boxer, only some muscles? Quite the contrary, he is at the same time a political being constantly alert to the horrifying, passionate or pleasing events in the world, shaping himself completely in their image. How is it possible to be uninterested in other men and by virtue of what cold nonchalance can you detach yourself from a life that they supply so copiously? No, painting is not made to decorate apartments. It's an offensive and defensive weapon against the enemy". (Téry, 1945). "If everyone would paint, political re-education would not be necessary". (Spender, 1946).

For, what will it be profitable for a man, if he gains the whole world and forfeits his life? Or what shall a man give in return for his life?

Jesus Christ

While performing art one has to be introspective.

Man is confined to a three-dimensional space, it's necessary to open a fourth dimension.

Working in lacquer, one is self-improving morally while painting.[1]

Painting a lacquer is like courting a beautiful lady,

---

(1) For more than 40 years since the time I started to learn to paint and to work on paintings, I've always asked myself: Why the Asian artists cannot reach the first-rate oil painting art like European, American and even Latin American artists? The answer is that the oil painting art originates from the Church, i.e. from the essence and spirit of Christianity, as right now the 20th century's contemporary plastic Arts still own a debt of gratitude to the Christ. The French masters have handed down to the Vietnamese students a mind-to-mind enlightenment on oil painting. Learning to paint, the learner has to perform art works and follow his master's view to perceive beauty. Since the 30s in the last century the masters had directed the students towards lacquer painting, and when the Vietnamese painters worked on lacquer, they had come back to the Orient, to their source as all three religions are one (Confucianism, Taoism, Buddhism) and had been the pioneers in Asia as well as in the world.

although one doesn't meet with her[1], but with one's presentiment and confidence, one has an unfaltering will to pursue one's aim.

One has to look with one's own eyes, while one must look at the lacquer with its own eyes, that is to say the lacquer's eyes.

One ought to learn Chinese characters.[2] The quintessence of Vietnamese classical poets resides in the Chinese characters. Sometimes they compose poems in Nôm (Demotic script) such as: Kiều, Cung Óan Ngâm Khúc (The history of Kiều, The Complaints of an Odalisque)... so as to permit the broad masses to better appreciate their works.

Language is also something that binds.

Working and reading too many things would pulverize one's strength. Looking with one's eyes and hearing with

---

(1) As Bodhidharma has said: "Once one has acquired the heart, one knows that no heart can be acquired. And once one has acquired the Way, one knows that no way can be acquired".

(2) When I talked about the Hinayana sutras that were newly translated into Vietnamese, he advised me to read Sino-Vietnamese sutras. He also told me that all important Buddhist sutras had been translated by the venerable bonzes to whom the Kings had given orders to do so. They are all Sino Vietnamese (or Sutras in demotics characters of the Vietnamese).

one's ears, each one of these matters has its own marvellous efficacity.

Confucianism cures skin diseases. Buddhism cures diseases in the marrow.

Filial piety in Buddhism is different from the one in Confucianism. Taking to religion is also a form of being reverent to one's parents, in this life as well as in former lives.

With lacquer, gold and silver aren't outward things.

Pay attention to the tiniest detail.

While painting, the fact of blotting out the flaws constitutes a means to set one's mind at rest, to train one's mind.

February 11, 1983

One would spoil oneself when using "black arts" skills.

All "black arts" aren't requirements by themselves. When using them, one is deceiving oneself, as well as deceiving other people.[1]

See note on page 73.

One must turn to difficult matters to study.

With regard to the lacquer's self-beauty, one must respect it. One ought to develop such a beauty and make it beautifuller.

Love accepts no reasoning. When loving, one loves all the beauties as well as all the defaults of the person one loves.

It's one's own mistake when getting entangled, it's not the mistakes of things.

By dint of painting florid works, later on, one can no longer paint great and serious works.

Conceiving a passion for wealth and glory is normal and common, but playing an exhibition game means taking a short cut.

There exists a kind of red brown that isn't transparent, and when being shined, it doesn't become brilliant. Upon wishing to use it, one must arrange previously its degree of dullness on the painting.

---

(1)While painting, at a certain stage, I experienced the technique of spraying petrol over the painting. He said so after looking at my work. He constantly wanted to use lacquer in a most unmixed way.

Upon painting matters with concrete shapes, one gets entangled in the figures. One has to escape from concrete matters. Pay attention only to materials and colours.

There exits in lacquer painting habits that cause one to get entangled in them, such as painting a multitude of trees to cover the spot on which a mistake is committed. Painting a wide levelled space is difficult as it's often interrupted.

Using materials, one must always ask oneself: can it be used in another way?

Constantly pay attention to the solidity and lastingness of the work. Beautifulness must go along with lastingness to produce a complete beautifulness.[1]

All researches, compositions, working methods have effects while working, once the work is realized, there will be no more effects.

No reasoning is involved, there are only love and passion.

---

(1) In 2000, I saw in musée Cernuschi de Paris an antique Chinese made lacquered bowl which had been produced in 480 BC. The bowl was still intact, as if almost 2500 years that had elapsed were like some dews sliding on it.

April 1, 1983

Painting is a kind of separate language. No one can use Man's language to refer to it.[1]

The painter doesn't ask any other person whether his work is beautiful or not, but, like a drinker drinking water, he must know all by himself whether it's hot or cold.

August 18, 1983

It would be weariful if all lacquers are similarly shining. Each one of the lacquers must have its own shining degree, different from other ones.[2]

Once the shine or levelness is obtained, one has to withdraw, looking for changes.[3]

---

(1) Art critic S. Hunter has written: "Art"... is something that has been discovered: it cannot be understood even by its creator".

(2) Poet Nguyễn Lương Ngọc has had a sharp-witted comment: he saw some of current lacquered paintings were "micacized (i.e. made micaceous), unlike those made of traditional lacquer, and insensible".

(3) Varnish resin-based lacquer left for a long time will become stonehard; to overcome its hardness, artists from the Indochina Fine Arts College have applied the flat sanding method. Under the surface of the product is a myriad of layers of paint, lines, and silver or gold inlaid. This is what referred to as "flat-painting lacquered work" by artists in South Vietnam. As for Nguyễn Gia Trí prior to 1945 in Hà Nội, he referred to lacquered work as "diamond sanding".

The shining degree must be as shining as possible when used for controlling scratches and levelness.

Reaching this stage, one no longer paints with one's eyes; one's hand perceives levelness more accurately than one's eyes.

One must head towards newness, towards freshness.

A new stage requires a new health, new cells. It requires a completely different man. Similar to an astronaut, one must be healthy and scholarly to be able to conduct the spaceship.

To reach a refined art, one must be hard to please.

The more the difficulty is, the more one's training oneself.

A lacquer painting can be intentionally uneven, but it must be usually smooth, passing beyond all unevenness.

A painting comes to a stop when it no longer brings to our mind anything new.

An art work has to endure inner compulsions in itself. Things outside it don't affect it, just like someone that observes a vegetarian diet.

Difficulty and favorableness are like the left foot and the right foot, when wishing to walk, one has to use both feet.

"Even in the underworld, the burden of my love will never be relieved" (Kiều).

Art is love. An unprecedented and unique love.

Painting is living and is different from illustrating. While painting one doesn't have any intention, the painting and oneself form a oneness.

Painting lacquer means striving to learn about the lacquer's rhythm of life. Each material has its own life. Lacquer has a slow rhythm, therefore, one can perceive it taking shape.

Dilute paint, thick paint, with a careless colour mixing, causing it to still have grains. The drop of paint that runs slantwise, or that runs straight, all have their own looks.

One ought to try to understand the materials as if one is trying to understand one's friends, one's lover, without forcing or oppressing the materials.

Each stroke depends on the vitality of the painter. When

one is weak, one paints in one manner, when one's is healthy, one paints differently. A broad-minded painter paints in a manner, a miserly painter paints in another manner. The painter's health is quite important.

Once one has understood, quick or slow doesn't make sense. A blink or one thousand years is the same, in connection with eternity. With time, a 100 years old man and a 3 years old child would be similar to each other.

Everything around us is abstract. The reason why we don't see these things is that because we always have in our inner-self a dictionary, keeping note of all our preconceived notions about these things, thus it impedes our ways of looking and thinking.

While painting, the painter and the painting is a oneness. When I say I paint, then I myself and the painting are divided into two elements. For that reason, producing is a lively activity that develops itself. Were one to observe a preconceived intention, then one is only illustrating the outer appearance.

The rhythm of lacquer is slow, it would be harmful to use light material such as silk. Just like when one is practicing weight–lifting then one cannot practice flying in the air.

November 10, 1983

Everything that is well-established is old. It's well-established because we've known about it beforehand.

One must live one's total life.

When producing, one always has a certain determination, while adopting a quite natural attitude, and the whole painting forms a unified slab.

One must answer to oneself, why one is painting like this, why one is painting like that, and why one is painting abstract? As everything can have an answer, and answering to oneself is the most difficult thing.

It's not the method, but it's the intention, from intention originates the method.

One must act contrarily to everything. All sense organs cannot be used.

Painting means communion. Upon saying "understood" one still stands outside.

One paints not because one likes to paint. The painting is a means leading to the directionless field.

One must reach a certain level to be able to understand the paintings in great museums.[1]

Each destiny has its own separation.

One sees God with one's heart, not with one's eyes.

The followers must undergo the sufferings of the Founder of the Religion to be able to sympathize with him.

When falling in love for the first time, one perceives that the world has another sex. When loving lacquer, one sees a new world, wide open before one's eyes.

The structures of temples involve particular rules and laws, and each one of them has its own signification. The Three- entrance Portico of the pagoda represents the Three Meditations: Meditation on Nothingness, Meditation on Shams, and Meditation on the Middle Way. It's open only to welcome blessed people, as for common people they'll have to use the Tổ (progenitor) gate behind the pagoda.

When producing, forget about vermilion, gold, silver,

---

(1) When I told him I wish to be allowed to see original works of world's masters, he answered me with this sentence. Ten years later, when I again expressed the desire to look at paintings of world's masters, he only told me "there's nothing to see at all".

eggshell. The mind and the materials form a oneness. Just like painting, Zen is a separate language which the laity cannot understand.

One enters into religion in order to become more clear-sighted, if failed to be so, one's act is useless.

Question: The Buddha, when enlightened under the Bodhi-tree, had worried about whether he should spread his teachings to people in the world or not. Thus, is it true that Buddha himself has to fight against his inner self?
Answer: The fight against one's inner self takes place until one's death, but it doesn't last a long time with someone that has reached the True Path.

One's mind constantly has the tendency to turn dry and stiff, to become a trail, this is something one has to blot out.

One cannot use language, which is limited, to deal with greater things.

Studying means living wholly one's social life, if limited within one's profession, one will be like the one that trains himself in martial art and, to have an acute hearing, poke his eyes and turn blind; this is a stupid way of training.

Pay attention to the tiniest dot.

When producing a new painting, one must know how to be "venturesome" and one must "dare to jump".

January 25, 1984

All contacts are harmful, even the one with one's teacher, if the contact isn't made with the right "precept". One's mind is a precious bulk of energy, but people use it mostly for useless matters. With things that become phenomena, that turn into physiognomies, one's mind has been worn away. Entering religion means acting exactly by contraries.

One must know how to concentrate all one's vitality on a unique aim: "enlightenment". Otherwise, it would be like boiling a water pot with a small fire,the water would become warm only. And the water might evaporate all by itself. At times, the pot becomes empty while the water isn't boiled yet.

Each painting is a "koàn", and constitutes a means to practice Zen.

An eggshell painting represents an equality between eggshell gold, silver and colour paints.

All creatures constantly multiply and change. If

something has a "physiognomy", it has detached itself from the whole.

One practices Yoga to preserve one's inner peace.

One must know how to feed one's mind. By dint of being used, one's mind will be torn up and exhausted. One must feed one's mind in a manner that could permit the painting, from the time it's roughed out to the time it's completed two or three years later, to remain fresh and lively, thus not being only a copy of the rough.

Only Buddha can break out of the three-dimensional space. [1]

One must train to use one's mind as a torchlight to give light to one's painting.

Working in lacquers is a way to reach self- understanding, and one can understand lacquer only when one understands oneself.

Sorrows are the seeds of Buddha.

---

(1) In the Three Greatest Men in History, English writer H.G.Wells (1866-1946) writes: "You see clearly a man, simple, devout, lonely, battling for light(...) Many of our best modern ideas are in closest harmony with it".

When left alone, the mind is white, when divided, it turns into hundreds of colours.

Don't distinguish capacity and preference. While painting, don't think one is painting. While painting, the most important thing is that the painter and the painting are one.

Preference or yearning is like a piece of paper. Capacity is like a fire, when burned, it becomes "void".

March 30, 1984

"The pure reason of one's essential nature is the precept".

Just like someone hit with a poisonous arrow. The most urgent thing is to extract that arrow.

Things that aren't finished on a painting, can only be known by the painter himself.

There is no particular idea, one has to let God's idea to bear rule.

Entering religion means one wishes to prove, to see. Therefore, one has to draw from one's inner self to see.

All easy solutions weaken oneself. The more the

288

difficulty exists, the more the progress is realized.[1]

One has to take great pains to see no great pains. In each painting reside the cause and effect.

Though one has one's belief, everything always seems like: *"...One let oneself go blindly on, just to see where fate would drive one to"*.

The more the religion is mighty, the more the evil spirits are flourishing.

Painting means exempting from griefs, the obstacles and griefs that grow bigger and bigger, created by oneself.

One is bound by one's own fame. Upon considering oneself as clever one can no longer progress.

Man's life, that has lasted millions of years, has turned many things into mechanical items. The King himself is a mechacical item.

While creating, if one fails to think and toss about, then

_____

(1) A. Camus has said something to the effect that: "One of A.Gide's statements may cause misunderstanding but I agree with him: "Art lives when it is constrained and dies when free". That is true... Art lives due to the constraints it imposes to itself... If art doesn't constrain itself, it would be delirious and would yield to unreal shadows".

one also turns into a mechanical person.

When plugged up while working in lacquers, one ought to change to other things: wood, oil, sculpture...

Although the painter is pure and clean, his work still has its own clamours.

All technical developments are due to the requirements of the painting, one doesn't have any previous intention.

Precept means one has turned into a precept, without knowing that one is precept itself.

Metamorphosing like geniuses.

One has no words, it's the Word.

One has an idea, then one paints accordingly to that idea, and that's an illustration.

One has to train until one can fly.

April 24, 1984

The "Void" in Buddhism isn't simple and easy. "Void" means no obstacle, no blockage. One cannot obtain such a "void" by means of sleeping a lot.

Beauty isn't beautiful. Beauty is the beauty of a mind, emitting light.

The light we see isn't the sunlight, or the electrical light, but it's the light of a mind that emits light.

Once one has painted and wants to continue to paint, one must join one's breath to the painting, allowing no separation.

The painting and the painter are one and cannot be divided into two.

Art reaching a high level is an art that cannot be turned over in one's mind. The one that can still be discussed is a mediocre one.

People conducting research work on Buddhism usually see only the outward appearance. As for the "marvelous efficacy", very few researchers can reach it, while this matter just cannot be taught. One that only speaks and doesn't cohabit with Truth, is simply a kind of "parrot".[1]

Performing art means swinging to and fro. Swinging to

---

(1) Catholic priest Thiện Cẩm also has written: "Buddha's teaching is a living philosophy. Because it is the Truth of Emancipation, only those who practise it could prove it and understand it. Otherwise, knowledge-based rationalization would only lead to blindly holding one's false belief".

and fro until one no longer sees, no longer knows, then lets go one's hands...

Black paint is precious because it's brazen and has the blue gleam of iron.

The *"Golden Mean"* is the only book of Confucianism that's readable.[1] Narrow-minded scholars always worry about punctilious matters.

Chinese art at its zenith was due to the influence of Zen. Buddhism is neither pessimistic, nor optimistic, but it seems like true.

A few things that go wrong in the materials can be accepted, if they are in keeping with the whole: as a fair whole is preferable to an outstanding part.

The painting has no subject. The main subject is the lacquer material.

There are things that cause one to repent throughout one's life...

The way to reach the True Path has many directions, many laws. Therefore, one can easily perish. The substance

---

(1) He may have forgotten the "I-Ching".

of the mind consists of three elements: wisdom, sentiment, and reason. When put to use the mind also involves three elements: dissipation of sorrows, confidence, and action. Confidence cannot be taught.

Painting is a law of causality, in which colours, drawings and time are fatefully brought together.

Space and time are one. Space can easily be seen, while time is difficult to perceive.

While performing art, one doesn't need to use one's will.

In painter J. Inguimberty's painting, a stroke includes everything, while describing the surface of a ricefield, in one of his stroke, we can see both the mud and the light.

Each artist has his own way of painting.

A painting contains many details, many styles, but they don't abuse one another.

All religions scratch out environments.

Were the eggshell to be hard, one has to continue to "hold sway over it".

With a painting, the beginning and the end are one.

One has to constantly connect one's breath, once done, the whole painting is a unique breath.

In a lacquer, when compared with red brown, black paint, and other colours such as vermilion, gold, silver, eggshell is quite a strange and somewhat hard material. Causing the eggshell to turn soft and harmonize lively with lacquer colours and materials is very difficult, one can say that it's the most difficult thing in the technique of lacquer producing.

May 9, 1984

One expects nothing from one's work.

It's of prime importance to the artist to avoid being conventional and worn out.

The main things in life are space and time. A painting is beautiful not because it's quickly or slowly done.

Working in a lacquer is like leaning on a crutch. If one cannot stand when leaving go of the crutch, then one is sick, one is a disabled person.

A lacquer that takes a long time to paint is like wine that has been covered for a long time, the longer the better.

Prayers and mind are one.

Buddha's strength is one thousand times more powerful than atomic energy. One has to believe in the marvellousness of Buddha's teachings.[1]

The completely beautiful painting is the one in which even the tiniest detail is beautiful, and filled with the breath of life.

Life is constantly beautiful, everything is beautiful.

Painting lacquer causes one to realize the most profound matters in one's heart of hearts. Taking to religion means happiness. If not, why would people take to religion.[2]

---

(1) Scientist A.Einstein has written: "The religion of the future will be a cosmic religion. It should transcend a personal God and avoid dogmas and theology. Covering both the natural and the spiritual, it should be based on a religious sense arising from the experience of all things, natural and spiritual, as a meaningful unity. Buddhism answers this description".

(2) The unique book painter Nguyễn Gia Trí gave to me and told me: "Keep it to muse upon" is the work entitled "Sáu cửa vào Động Thiếu Thất" (Six gates leading to the Thiếu Thất grotto) by Bodhidharma and translated by Trúc Thiên. In this book he red-pencilled the following sentence: "Seeing the presence of forms means being constantly bound. Not being bound by sorrows means being freed from sorrows, and there exists no other deliverance".

Having honours and interests is also a misfortune.[1]

The more religion is powerful, the more evil spirits flourish. For example, one is 10 metres high, then it's 20 metres high.

While taking to religion and training oneself, one must act harmoniously and naturally. When being too repressed *"instead of gaining strength, one might suffer from an internal lesion"*.

A talented artist is always lonely. It's a rare thing to have an intimate friend.

One should have only a skimming look at outward things. One shouldn't scrutinize deeply into some meanness, just save this scrutiny for oneself.

Some people like to practice divination, and thus are indulged in vain hopes: they know everything, except for knowing about themselves.

Art is aimed at reaching a beauty as light as a breath, without requiring much effort. Like with heaven and earth,

---

(1) *"Wei shan's Switch" reads: "Fame and wealth are like dust in one's eyes".*

a storm, a lightning, is also quite soft.[1]

The reason for which the painting causes one to feel flustered is that one has spent too much effort on it.

Ordinary people don't realize they're living in misery.

One is confident and can take to religion as one withstands lacquer.

Picasso's change is a change in depth.

A genuinely producing artist doesn't adopt any school. The history of art is owing to art critics that classify.

A painting one is striving to make it beautiful, will become an unsightly one.

A consistent painting is a painting in which everything follows a same law. If the painter is consistent, the painting is also consistent.

---

(1) Van Gogh once said: "I envy the Japanese artists for the incredible neat clarity which all their works have. It is never boring and you never get the impression that they work in a hurry. It is as simple as breathing; they draw a figure with a couple of strokes with such an unfailing easiness as if it were as easy as buttoning one's waist-coat".

Upon taking to religion, one realizes that the past is quite a burden.

All sense organs are means and are at the same time obstacles.

Misery and happiness are not given to any particular person by Buddha, as Buddha has compassion for everybody.

June 6, 1984

The artist looks for truth. This truth is out of time. It might exist before mankind came into existence.

Art exceeds all treatments, truthfulness, admiration.

Painting means revealing one's mind and displaying it.

Taking to religion means reforming, but the reform must be rightly understood, otherwise everything will be askew.

The painter's mind is the inward expression while painting, as for looking for it on the surface of the painting, it's meaningless most of the times.

Abstract painting is the style that is most close to

one's mind, as it's free, unbound.

While performing art, the artist is looking for that "divine intervention". The use of that "divine intervention" surpasses the body and is out of, and beyond the body.[1]

Art through which one still can see the profile of the painter, is an art of the lowest quality.[2]

When one is sick, it's one's body that is sick, one's mind, one's spirit, aren't sick at all.

The artist uses his mind to project outwardly *"casting his idea"* like an electrical beam. Or, similar to a blindman, using his stick to sound his way, upon meeting with an obstacle, he withdraws it.

---

(1) A passage from the "Suramgama Sutra" reads: "Throughout the ten directions of the world is the eye of the Buddhist monk! Throughout the ten directions of the world is the Buddhist monk's whole body!" (Translated by venerable bonze Nhẫn Tế).
The Russian Rev. Father, who is also a scholar and a philosopher P.A. Florensky (1882-1943) has written about Andrei Rublev's Trinity, the most famous of all Russian icons, as follows: "Among all the philosophical proofs of God's existence, the most forceful one isn't mentioned in any textbook, and it can be summarized as follows: "The Trinity painting by Rublev exists, thus it means that God exists".
(2) One day while looking at the photographs of bas-reliefs in the ancient art of Borobodur (Indonesia),he told me: "Believing that these are man-made things is a big mistake".

Big is one's mind that has neither interior, nor exterior.

Things that look simple, ordinary, are genuine ones. Things that have styles and are decorated, are unreal ones.

Taking to religion and training oneself, sometimes the results are unbounded and unforeseeable. If seeing only a result in the lacquer,then it's really too small.

With the Yiking, when applied to divination, one is having something really small, like flowers or fruits on a tree. There exists a big difference between divination and abstract painting. From the divination side, one bases oneself on rules and experiences to determine the result. As for the painting, one is doing exactly the contrary, and doesn't need any result.

When taking to religion,or performing art, one ought to be easy, natural, as it would be no good to deploy too much effort and be too sluggish. It isn't good enough when one still has to shilly-shally.

When wishing to take to religion, one must have a pre-disposition, and a deep-rooted one.

Among the numbers 1, 2, 3 and 0, number 3 is the biggest one.

Wishing to have one's paintings exposed in Paris means cherishing a hope. Living with a sham thing is harmful for the source.

The cake is tasty because of leaven.

July 4, 1984

Vermilion that overflows the interstices of eggshell is like waters from rivers, canals, that are similar everywhere.

A stroke also contains eggshell substance.

In an eggshell painting, all parts have the same good results of eggshell.

Push to crush the eggshell, and move the eggshell while the paint is still wet.

Painting abstract means destroying the physiognomy, to see the physionomy without physiognomy.

The particles of eggshell that lie on the vermilion base are like mountain crests emerging from the sea.

Dividing time into present, past, future, is also a mechanical action.

July 5, 1984

One has to go through the "change" to be able to reach "constancy".

Thing that is stiff can be broken, a big tree can be uprooted in a big storm.

On an eggshell painting, the cracks are big or small is a matter that depends on the sizes of the painting.

The development of vital spirit always involve leaps and bounds.

The lives of old and young people are different, therefore their arts are also different.

The main difficulty resides in the fact that, although great pains have been taken, everything still seems like very easy.

When wishing to use an artisan, one has to constantly train him, as well as to constantly change and promote the artisan's ability.

July 8, 1984

There exist Zen "koàn" (A puzzling, often paradoxical

stalement used in Zen Buddhism) that require the student to cudgel his brains. Cudgeling one's brains to infer, to argue, so as to make something else clear.

When thinking and working, one cannot stick to a happy medium, and cannot be regular, as by acting so, everything will little by little turn into mechanical matters.

One lives to become natural like trees and grass, but the kind of trees and grass that know how to think.

Each obstacle is a door. Only by passing through one door,can one reach another one.

The real teaching is the one beyond academic books. One has to actually start working.

One shouldn't let oneself turn into a "satellite"[1], even though one might be the "satellite" of a holy man. However, there must always be some "encircling"[2], even the Great Bear also has an "encircling".

Life and death are one, to understand and catch hold of life and death, one must stay outside of life and death.

---

(1) Triển: an encircling.
(2) Painter Nguyễn Sáng also said: "each artist must be a planet, and cannot be the satellite of anyone".

303

"The Complaints of an Odalisk" refers to the ties that bound man's life. The artist is similar to the odalisk who constantly awaits for the arrival of her heart's king. When young and filled with creativities and inspirations, she was frequently visited by the king, so she was all fresh and happy. Upon becoming older, her king's visits turn scarcer and scarcer. The artist 's old paintings and sketches are like the Odalisk's ancient attire in days past, that remained after her meeting with the king.[1]

A beautiful painting must be "full of life", without the "fullness of life", the painting just couldn't be beautiful.

When learning how to paint, one must train oneself to paint quickly so as to catch hold of the "liveliness". But, there exist people that paint quickly, or slowly, while they still cannot catch hold of any "liveliness".

"Liveliness" reveals itself to us immediately, even faster than the twinkling of an eye.

The pleasantness of a poem resides in the fact that it doesn't deal with anything concrete.

---

(1) Then he added: "I'm now like an old odalisk "tilting the mildewed powder box to make up my wrinkled cheek". He's constantly simple and modest, at times he cracked jokes naturally, creating equality and giving confidence to his students.

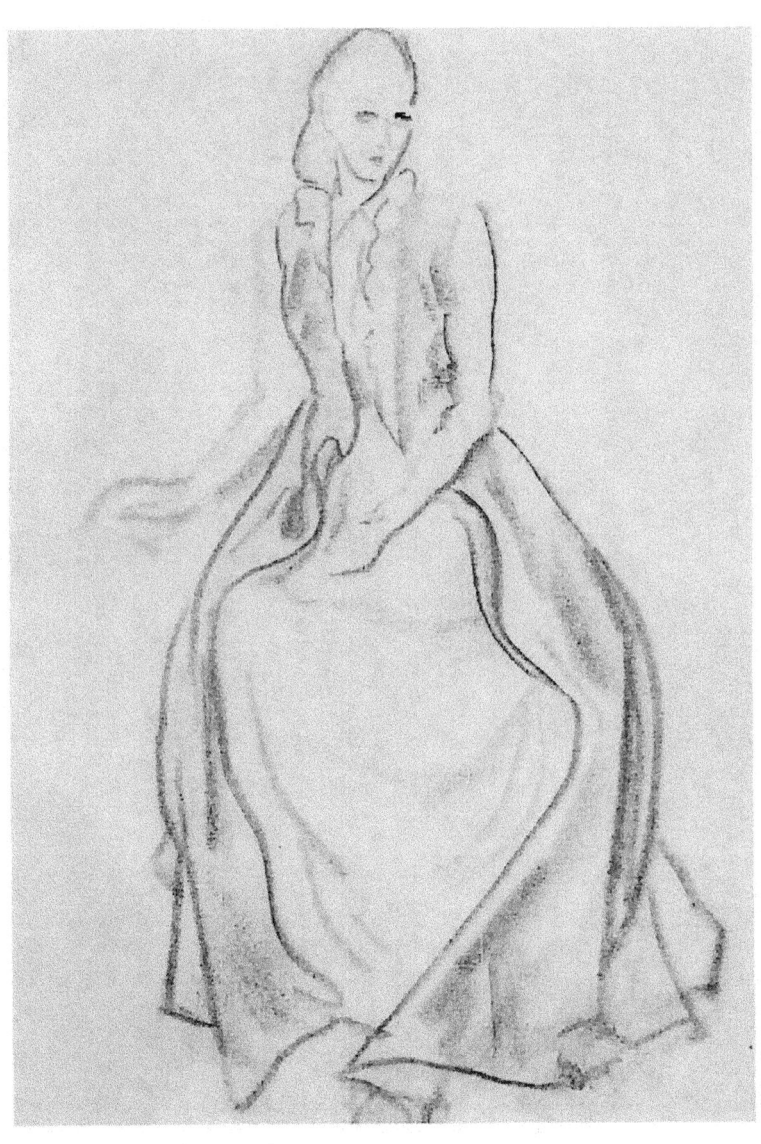

Tranh "Thiếu nữ Pháp" (0m27x0m20) than của họa sĩ Nguyễn Gia Trí
"A French woman" sketch by artist Nguyễn Gia Trí

.

One must learn to catch hold of the plastic art language. There exists the type of direct language, as well as the type of indirect language, expressed through a story, or a philosophy.

Not "revealing one's virtues" means not being hypocrite, or solemn. One shouldn't show one's talent, as it's harmful and lessens one's energy.

If one only works in oil paints, and doesn't work in lacquer, then one cannot "escape".

Talking about Zen, doesn't mean that it's Zen. Sitting in meditation isn't enough. Carrying water, chopping wood also mean practising Zen.

While painting, don't be obstinate. With each painting, even though one has had preparations and anticipations, the painting will not appear as one has anticipated. Thus, one has to be adaptable and take it the way it is.

When wishing to be free, one has to leave one's life as a deposit.

"Father, I'll comply with your idea", I'll do exactly what you want me to do.

Being rich, while not knowing to use one's wealth to

engage in benevolent action, is also a karmaic effect.

One must not identify oneself with the universe, but one must get on well with it, while standing out of it, and standing out of life and death. As life and death are false, dim-sighted, inflamed.

One has to release and forsake, and the things one releases and forsakes cannot be seen.

One must feel and perceive everything all by oneself, one cannot rely only on books and knowledge.

Life, nature, are dim-sighted, inflamed, speckled flowers, there exist things that are beautiful. Life also means practicing a religion.

Picasso had destroyed the features, but the features are boundless.

The artist is both inside and outside of the painting, even in each crack of eggshell.

The void in the air and the void under the water are always the void.

There is only the "unanimity" that turns into a variety when being analyzed.

One cannot run after life for ever.

With things that are easy to see, to look at, one is often mistaken. It's very difficult for the artist to be mistaken, as he's in direct contact with the painting.

One cannot adopt a manner forever, as it'll become something mechanic.

One's heart must remain fresh.

Practicing a religion at a certain degree, one will perceive that there is no death, and death is only a sham.

A broken foot, a broken arm, a sick body can be seen easily. A suffering, a broken,and a dead heart, no one can see.

There exists the Buddha that is active, as well as the Buddha that only sits in the pagoda. There are Buddhas that have white skin, yellow skin and black skin.

I like Thai Buddhist painting more than Japanese Buddhist painting.

July 21, 1984

The king of heart has only one heart.

There are people that never heard about or knew the king of heart, all the more meeting him.

With art, the laws and regulations are established by one oneself, so there is nothing to be afraid of.

Each artist makes the best of the paint accordingly to his own method.

"Not joining the unhallowed holy men from a same encircling,
Passing beyond all of them to come up and call oneself Patron Saint".

Bodhiharma

If one fails to free, to liberate oneself, one will be subject to metempsychosis.

Things one has the knack of doing will become something mechanic.

Working in lacquer, if one continues to produce handicraft products, one will never be able to make one's way in life. One must secure big customers, of international stature such as some oil kings.

Intellectualism is a complicated teaching. It's for consulting like a dictionary only. The artist always acts inversely. He produces first, then learns and learns in his own manner.

Question: The scriptures of religions often deal with the term "alien". What's meant by "alien?".
Answer: "Alien" to religion are "matters" that are opposed to one's mind, to one's religion that lies in one's inner self.

One must always renounce oneself. Forget all what one has done and continue to march forward, only by doing so, can one perceive the new.

Countries that are far from the True Path are the ones that live on top. People that are near the Truth Path are people living at the base[1].

Socrates has said: "Know thyself".

Whatever one's nature is, it will be faithfully materialized. It might be brutish, awkward or refined...

---

1) Zen Buddhist bonze Tai Hui(1088-1163) has said: "Once one has the base, one doesn't have to worry about the top. Cleaning one's heart means one has acquired the base, and then all languages, all wisdoms will, depending on the act of God, be received daily. Completely upset, angry or happy, good or bad, for and against, all such conditions belong in the top. If, through the act of God, one can maintain one's true self, then with one, everything will neither be lacking, nor superabundant!".

When studying and reading, one must have digestion. It would be detrimental to eat and have no digestion, as one's stomach will contain only rice.

One's mind includes: intelligence, sentiment, idea. Its deployment consists of: liberation, belief, and action.. Art means sentiment and belief, not intelligence. However, such factors always intermingle with one another.

Life and death are one. Death is only a slumber, one will see oneself awakened the following morning.

Working in lacquer is aimed at understanding its vital rhythm. There must be an agreement between the painter and the painting.

A passage in the Maitreya Sutra reads: "Nirvana is in one's inner self and is built by oneself, it isn't at the exterior. It isn't true that one will die then leave this world for another place".

The deployment of one's mind is soft and changing. One has to deploy and train to know.

One's "ego" is like a contour[1] in classic painting. It separates one from other people.

---

(1) The outline of the painting.

One's talent for painting is used to paint the "void-nothingness".

Were one to know, one will see that one has given birth to creatures. Colours don't really exist, and the unique colour is white, the black colour also doesn't exist.

The term "Cúng Dường" (consecrated to the Buddha) also means "Cung Dưỡng" (Providing and rearing) i.e. rearing one's mind.

The contour changes its shades from dark to light, depending on the changes in one's mind.

Picasso also has a religion, his own religion. Without religion, one simply cannot escape.

Strokes and features spring from one's heart of hearts, were it to spring only from one's mind, then it will be insensible and stiff.

The smoothness of lacquer is a lively smoothness. If produced by a machine, it will not bear any significance.

Producing means the artist is identified with the painting, while another identification also develops in the artist's mind.

If a painter is talented, it's thanks to his eyes, not to his two hands. The hidden self is good, but the revealing self is no good.

A poem has a certain dimness, influencing the ideas and figures. If the figures are too clear cut, they are detrimental to its refined and uncanny nature. If it's too refined and uncanny, then it's detrimental to the figures.

Painting, writing, or speaking, if one doesn't use these matters quite often in deep areas in one's mind, then they would be difficult to know and to use.

A millions and millions years old star and a new born star, with its new light, can be seen equally by people.

A painting work is similar to the currency of a nation. And the artist's signature is aimed at acknowledging the value of that currency, not allowing it to suffer from an inflation.

People that are "stagy", or overtly affected, are simply superficial and frivolous.

When wishing to meet with God, one at first has to atone for one's sins.

The "void–nothingness" of Buddhism is also everything.

Eating in a spiritual way, as well as actually eating, are also eating. One's body is also one's spirit.

Being an artist, one of course write beautiful chinese characters, even one's writing with a broom.

The artful painter is the one that can paint the "void-nothingness".

August 13, 1984

Buddha has taught that one must avoid being renowned and charming people.

While taking to religion, one might very well go astray.

Question: Why Bodhidharma once said: "As soon as one has some public virtues, one is immediately pursued by murkiness?"
Answer: "Murkiness is our own one, engendered by proudness in our heart. Everything is owing to our heart".

Ghosts also have their own cleverness.[1]

---

(1) With that, he recited a Buddhist legend for an example: "Once there was a most venerable bonze who was enlightened, living in the mountains. He caught a ghost and he wanted to challenge its skills. He told the ghost: "You shall perform a miracle that I could see the Buddha and His 1250 disciples as when they were alive". The ghost managed to do it. Seeing the Buddha and His 1250 disciplines standing in bright halo, the most venerable monk bowed and prostrated himself before them".
The Christians also mention Satan who could perform almost everything done by God, except the only thing that it cannot create life.

September 5, 1984

The problem isn't whether one is well learned or not, but, from a small point,were one to dig deeper and deeper, one will find it. Like when one polishes continually at a same spot, one will reach the wood panel.

One isn't intelligent enough to do evil.

With a painting, everything will be all right if the questions of lay-out and technique have been solved.

Concerning one's good manners, one has to observe the criteria of the sutra, otherwise one might make mistakes. Buddhism doesn't mention the time, but there is constantly a time, a super time.

"*One has carried one's cry and one's head with both hands to come out*". Carrying one's head with both hands is neat, so one can come out, with hands stretched out, one cannot come out.

Dream isn't real. The painter himself has painted a dream, then deleted it.

Everything must be authorized by one's heart of hearts.

I created with my presentiment.

314

September 20, 1984

One's technique is supposed to be intentional, but it has to remain natural, harmonious, seeming like unintentional.

When swinging to and fro and jumping, one doesn't know at all, it's only because one is confident that one can catch hold of the other side. Were one to think while at the middle of the distance,one would fall down.

Draw a red and flat base beside the eggshell, one will perceive a particular effect, and this constitutes a way of training.

The Enlightenment state is almost like letting fall a plank.[1] It happened so quick that one had no time to react, as quick as a lightning, upon recalling, one saw it dimly. A Buddhist Zen bonze was sweeping a courtyard, a pebble shot forth at the root of a bamboo tree, emitting a sound, and he was suddenly enlightened.

Among different religious practices, Mahayanism is the most difficult one.

---

(1) At 80 he was still working on the work entitle "Centre of South and North Spring Garden"; one day in his workshop, he raised a plank, let fall it, and had his wrist bone broken, and he had talked about "enlightenment" like this.

All kinds of ghosts have their origin in one's soul.

The ghosts are the books one has read, the death formulae and corrupt manners, such things obstruct one's actual life.[1]

I work in lacquer since it first appeared, so my age is the same with the age of lacquer. I live with it like a fish with water, so I don't know that I'm living. Only the onlookers can see and perceive.

The public is an insatiable devil, that constantly wants to devour the artist. Like in a theatrical performance, they shouted "again", "again", "again". The artist has to remain lucid to preserve his creative capacity.

When painting, one has a stay that preserves our soul from turning mad. The devils cannot make an attempt on one's life.

---

(1) Picasso compared the work of madmen and the death: "The work of madmen", he told me, "is always based on a law that has ceased to operate. Madmen are men who have lost their imagination. Their manual memory belongs to a realm of rigid mechanism. It is an infernal machine that breaks down and not an intelligence that progresses and constantly creates in order to progress. One cannot compare poems resulting from automatic writing with those of the insane. The work of a madman is a dead work; the poetry it contains is like the ghost which refuses to give up its corpse". (Parrot, 1948, page 8).

One's training and one's painting have no time limit, it would be the same were one to spend 2-3 years or 10 years to paint.

October 25, 1984

The attitude of the religious is to avoid all disputes. Whatever the religious does must be a good deed. A religious never has a "learning" towards any side.

Keeping silence is the best solution, the more one talks, the more one's ignorance is proven.

Lacquer is a local product of Vietnam. *"Indivisible is one's life and one's land"*, and such a fact brings about a great vitality.

Lacquer is a means for the artist to live and think. If he fails to actually live with it, then, even though he might paint a painting as big as the Tu Di mountain, he still doesn't have any merit.

Technique isn't difficult. The fundamental question is that one must solve it as a whole.

The question is to have confidence and to believe. One can talk about believing only with someone with a religious faith. Otherwise, it'll be just like talking about light and colours with a blind man.[1]

When the Bodhisattva of Endless Idea gave the most precious thing to the Bodhisattva of Compassion and Love (Avalokitesvara), She had asked for the Buddha's opinion, and had received only after Buddha had agreed.

The capacity of lacquer can change endlessly. One shouldn't be bound by any formula.

One paints, not for the sake of anything, not for the sake of the painter, or of the work itself.[2]

One expects nothing from one's work.

A tiny grain of paint contains everything. When someone splashes a drop of ink on a piece of paper, a man with a deep knowledge can read that person's character, his intention and his thoughts.

---

(1) A. Liberman: "Cézanne vision was close to that of another mystic, Spinoza, who wrote: "God and the universal laws of structure and operation are one and the same reality". Cézanne's answer to a friend who asked him if he believed was "If I did not believe I could not paint".
(2) Artist Bùi Xuân Phái said: "It you paint for something, you would fluff the painting".

Train one's mind to know about everything (Know all mind).[1]

The artist is like a child, nosing about and playing with his own work.

"One deliberately plant flowers, flowers are withering, One unintentionally puts some willow-trees into the ground, the willow-trees turn luxuriant".

November 10, 1984

One has to live out of the control of one's body and sense organs.

One's painting isn't based on figures, colours, but on materials and one's heart of hearts.

Things that are dead, that belong in the past, are "ghost", mere corpses.

One has to bear testimony to one's enlightenment.

Practicing religion, one has to understand action

---

(1) *Bonze Thuận Thiện explained: "Everything is created by one heart of hearts, thus knowing one's heart of hearts means knowing everything".*

319

through another meaning. Action doesn't mean having to act, but sitting still is also action.

A painting is like a raft used for crossing a river, after the crossing one discards it, without a raft one can walk on foot.

While practicing a religion, one is like a mountain climber, or someone who is curing a disease. Zen means climbing one hundred metres up to the top of a pole, then proceed with an additional step...

Cleverness slows down the development. It's the hard outer cover that bundles, not permitting anything to get inside, like a husk.

All contacts are polluted. "Dropping one's arms to enter the market", is aimed at gaining more strength, more food for practicing religion, not for inconsiderately doing business.

The relation between the painter and the painting is like the one of two friends.

Practing religion means heading towards the origin, towards the source of Cam Lồ (Amrta) water to drink, so one remains young and fresh forever.

While painting,, one wishes 10 years to be like one

hour. A panel that weighs a hundred kilos to be like weight-less.

Lao-ji once said: *"When succeeding in one's studies, one fails in one's religious practices"*.

November 20, 1984

A genuine True Path doesn't need preaching and propaganda. The more one preaches, the greater and the distance, and the more one tarnishes it.

One has to live substantially to understand lacquer, and this is the relation between man and painting, and one cannot have a leaning towards any side.

Practicing a religion means Listening, Meditating, and Going into action. One has to meditate in order to have a mind of deep insight.

All matters on the painting must be transformed into one. One cannot add up 3 eggs to 2 guavas and 5 mangoes.

All such matters must be converted into money, then add up. The amount will be decided upon accordingly to one's heart.

The enlightenment of each person occurs accordingly

to his own manner. The True Path has no formula and no appearance.

The True Path is like a sheet of white linen, once used, it loses its original aspect. Once cut to pieces, it can no longer be mended as before. A dot made by a needle point always leaves a trace.

It's infinite when one chooses the top, going back to the source, one'll have everything.

February 5, 1985

Genuine art causes the person that creates it to be transformed.

Working in lacquer is aimed at catching hold of the main point. What's the basic difference between oil and lacquer paintings? One has to ask the process one has gone through oneself. If failing to state questions, to become anxious and to think, then, although one might paint for 10 years, or 20 years, no change will ever occur. The difference between lacquer and oil paint resides in the lacquerer's diligent studies and good execution.[1]

See note on page 119.

There exists no leisure and easy way in art.

The most essential thing is "enlightenment".

Working in lacquer isn't for re-illustrating the history of oil paint.

The forthcoming process will lead to obstruction.

---

(1) With the devoted teaching of two talented teachers: painter V. Tardieu and painter J. Inguimberty, the Vietnamese painters graduated from the Indochina School of Fine Arts, have studied all the techniques and creative concepts of Occidental oil painting, that has undergone a process of development amounting to almost 600 years.

The french famous painter Courbet has written: "Art doesn't originate from zero, it goes from conclusion to conclusion". One can say: "In a period of time of more than half of a century, the Vietnamese painters have gone through the conclusions of the essence of occidental oil paint and the technique of Japanese traditional lacquer, to create the use of the "lacquer", an indigenous material of Vietnam and Asia, transforming it into a modern plastic art material bearing an international common value.

The Vietnamese painters that have greatly contributed to the development of lacquer are: Trần Quang Trân, Phạm Hậu, Nguyễn Văn Quế, Lê Quốc Lộc, Nguyễn Văn Ty, Hoàng Tich Chù, Nguyễn Tiến Chung, Tô ngọc Vân, Trần Văn Cẩn, Kim Đồng, Sĩ Ngọc, Nguyễn Tư Nghiêm, Nguyễn Sáng and at the summit, Nguyễn Gia Trí.

His works have become elaborated, and he has transformed lacquer materials into artistic items with a limitless spiritual content. Originating from the 1000 years old Thăng Long, in 1935, with the artistic lacquer works, the Vietnamese painters have created the playing rule for the "Flat world" that corresponds to the Buddhist prayer: "Everything are on equal terms, there exist no higher or lower things".

Picasso was obstructed when he shifted to working in pottery.

The Dhamma is something very difficult, very hard. I broke my arms and my leg, yet I still couldn't find it. I must have a Master who breaks my head, then maybe I'll understand.

A painting is a direct expression by means of the plastic art.

I like Thai buddhistic painting more than Japanese buddhistic painting.

February 20, 1985

The greatest problem in a man's life consists of reaching: "Enlightenment".

Lacquer is a narrow gate leading to a much larger space.

Great pains mean unifying ability and desire, so as to transform them into whole-heartedness. If only technique and ability are involved, thing will turn mechanic.

Harmonize between thinking and painting. Thinking

without painting means insignificant thinking. Painting without thinking of the results obtained, means working in a mechanical manner.

If it's only an accidental technique, then no effect is involved. The problem consists of solving things that are in one's inner feelings.

One's concentration on one point would cause one's inner feelings to calm down. When one is half-awakened, half slept, one is in a coma.

Living without clearing the obstactles on one's way to "Enlightenment" is living a wasted life. Having an appointment with future life means a lot of misfortunes.[1]

The question of breathing is very important. An

---

(1) The Verse for opening the Vajra Sùtra reads: "The unsurpassed, deep, profound, subtle wonderful Dharma. In a hundred thousand million eons, it is difficult to encounter. Now that I have come to receive and hold it, within my sight and hearing. I vow to fathom the Thus Come One's true and actual meaning". In the Vajracchedika Prajnaparamita Sutra, the Buddha said: "Subhuti. if as many times as there are grains of sand in the Ganges a son or daughter of a good family gives up his or her life as an act of generosity and if another daughter or son of a good family knows how to accept, practice, and explain this sutra to others, even if only a gatha of four lines, the happiness resulting from explaining this sutra is far greater". The core of Buddhism is our mind reaching Enlightenment.

embryonic foetus is like a fish in water, upon being delivered, the midwife had to slab its rump before it could breathe.

Upon taking to religion one progresses gradually, but when reaching enlightenment, one is subject to a suddenness. At times, one even reaches enlightenment before taking to religion.

Technique, cleverness can be obtained by a long training, but hard pains are different.

In the process of producing,there are diseases that got lost, one never knows when.

March 7, 1985

Everything begins with one's mental conception, whatever it might be, one is exactly like it.

Paying too much attention to the environment, one'll lose one's personality, and will be subject to metempsychosis forever.

Religion is mighty, but evil spirits are also flourishing, practicing religion becomes more and more difficult.

The place where the saint patron of lacquer Trần Tướng Công[1] is worshipped is the Bình Vọng village.

A painting must have some liveliness, without it the painting cannot be achieved.

One's mental conception when starting to produce is usually insignificant. One is like someone feeling his way in the dark, it's the working process that leads to beauty. With time, the painting's space turns larger and larger. The most important thing is the working process.

April 1, 1985

Changes are involved only when one paints quickly. The changes in the eggshell occur very slowly.

One has to learn to walk, bending one's body within a frame, then later on, one'll be able to tiptoe.

Using a pencil to draw is a way of practicing to paint nature in a most secure way.

Genuine learning must be something that has

---

(1) As advised by villagers, the name of the painting progenitor has been engraved on a stele in National Literary Temple.

undergone, several generations, several lives. The concrete academic learning isn't of any account.

Practicing Zen is aimed at remaining clear-minded, clear-sighted, to head towards Enlightenment, not for slumbering with a peaceful mind.

The firmness obtained through training is the most secure one.

Most important of all is the working process. Once the painting is achieved,the result is obtained. It's not suitable to constantly expect good results.

While working, one often accumulate many new things.

One used to consider all problems through one's profession.

Asked: What is a reasonable price that should be put on the tag for a painting?
Answered: An artist has the right to decide the prices for his paintings and he also has the right to abstain from food...

April 27, 1985

One usually doesn't use up one's wisdom, one often uses it partially only, when using up one's wisdom, the effect will be really great.

The Saddharmapundarika - Sutra is the basic canonical book of Buddhism.

The painter uses his eyes to work and is also obstructed by his own eyes. Lacquer causes this obstruction to be changed. Painting lacquer, one at times is like a carpenter, at other times, is like a ploughing peasant.

Collage teaches one many other things than copying down nature.

The artist is all by himself and doesn't need anyone to "appreciate" him.

The artist constantly frees himself from familiar and social bondage.

One doesn't paint in the classical way, as one has changed. One just cannot withdraw and has to be in agreement with the impulse.

Lacquer helps one to develop in many aspects, both spiritual and material.

While producing, the best thing is to work regularly, as when stopping for a long time, it will be real hard to restart.

May 3, 1985

Doing artwork, one cannot rely on one's "intelligence" to protect oneself.

One has to concentrate on a unique work, like one is continually hollowing out a door, then later on, one will be able to escape. Were one to try one thing, then another thing, as a result, nothing could be done correctly.

One must always remember: One's painting is only a means to train oneself.

One must make use of one's mind in a gentle manner. Leaving it in peace also constitutes a working method.

Paint directly on the "vóc" (a board covered with a cloth on which is spread a layer of lacquer).

July 8, 1985

Life is one. As people divide it into hundreds of things, thus it's broken into smithereens.

Mandala[1] builds his own statue and use it to cure his own diseases.

_____

(1) According to Mahàyanà Buddhism, the Mantra Sect represents the universe

330

Painting abstract or painting anything, depends on one's requirements.

Question: "What are the meaning of permanency, happiness, ego and pureness?"
Answer: (He didn't answer and kept silent while bending his head), then, a moment later, he said: "One recites the Mahaøparinirvana-sutra only when one's about to die".

Question: A passage in the Buddhist canonical book reads: "Practicing religion is like a log floating on the river, if it doesn't go astray, or be driven to the shore, it'll flow out to the sea", what does this passage mean?
Answer: Even drifted to the sea, the log is still the log. I hate reading fastidious canonical books.

July 17, 1985

While working in lacquer, the main thing is how one's hard pains effect one's inner feelings. One has to proceed in this way to be able to meet with Enlightenment.

Working in lacquer is to have a knowledge of its character. Don't impose anything it doesn't possess. Were one to wish to have many colours, then one should work in oil paint. Actually, one's mind doesn't have many colours.[1]

---

(1) Picasso has also said: Painting with multi-colours the images would be dull. Artist NGUYỄN SÁNG said: "THERE ARE NO COLOURS, THERE IS ONLY LIGHT".

331

A shining and smooth lacquer also represents much hard pains.

After achieving a painting, one asks oneself whether one is satisfying or not,then one will know.

Being "*at leisure*" is also a Zen practice.

The "Hương" (Perfume) pagoda loses its beauty when being turned into a touristic sight. It also loses its traditional and sacred aspect.

Act naturally, without any calculation, and one's reaching the True Path.

Everything is false, only the True Path is genuine.[1]

Jumping across an abyss is taking a risk. But, upon training oneself to jump, one must have something to prop one up. Each painting is a risk taken. But if one doesn't take any risk, one never obtains anything new.

---

(1) Bodhidharma once said: "There isn't a thing since days of yore up to now, to say nothing of two falseness".
H.G.Wells once wrote: "Before a man can become serene he must cease to live for his senses or himself.
Then he merges into a great being".

While working in lacquer, one understands and sees one's mind, which is something one doesn't see and cannot catch.

Fakery is something involving no cleverness, something clumsy.[1]

Each artist has an obsession for him to personally pursue, ahead of him.

Learning from an artist, is learning about his past working process, but not imitating his form, that is an appearance.

A pagoda must have religious, and pilgrims from everywhere that come to worship, to be considered as a sacred one.

August 9, 1985

Lacquer has no area. The artist's mission consists of destroying all limits.

---

(1) He said this when I asked him about the type of painting that looks fairly beautiful and cleverly done, but the artist's personality is quite mediocre. Painter Nguyễn Sáng also said: "Art has no second class, it's either gold or it's grass".

Matisse is one among the explorers of new space.

Even in the cosmos, it's also a three-dimension space.

Paintings by European artists have a light spiritual nature, as their philosophy is light,their methods are inclined towards outer appearance.[1]

Looking at books on painting makes one go crazy.

Paintings with figures mean foreseen sketches are involved. Abstract paintings are exactly the contrary of the above- mentioned remark.

Paintings are tools for curing diseases.

Upon sitting and thinking of the painting, one's also penetrating the true essence of one's self.

The bigger the painting, the more one's strength can easily be wasted.

Breaking means breaking the obstinateness of form. Form cannot be destroyed. One breaks this pattern, it becomes another pattern.

---

(1) Thus said he when I compared the original lines made by artist Hokusai with those by European ones.

The unsightliness and the beautiful don't reside in the form, as beauty resides in another place.

Form without form is the actual form.

Asian aesthetic sense prefers soft and perky thing and dislikes anything ponderous.

One must verify everything all by oneself.

One's knowledge and competency also constitute a kind of ghost.

October 7, 1985

Zen Masters constantly remind their disciples: not to mistake means for ends.[1]

While practicing religion, if one still has doubts, then one hasn't arrive yet. Like a grain of dust falling into a machinery, or a drop of water dropping into a gasoline can, causing such things to turn incomplete.

---

(1) Poet O. Paz one said: "Something to the effect that: Alienation - I think the alienation is really in the way we worship means, and see it as our end. We glorify our cars, our TVs... That's why our world has lost its meanings. Isn't that important, when we have become enslaved to our means?"

The beauty of the painting includes many criteria, one among them must be given particular attention: it must be lasting to reach everlastingness.

Art is idealistic.

The artist is a man with a pair of hands that turn everything that touch into gold.

A poem is good because it has something that's lasting, and that thing is its lyrical inspiration, that escapes from sounds and words that are things that aren't lasting. This is because the sounds and words are read differently in each one of the countries in the world.

At times, Picasso transformed art into magic.

One reaches self-enlightenment when one comes to a dead end, between life and death.

As we artists belong in mankind, we're living the ordinary life of Man with problems such as marriage, having children.

When still young, one has to work with a method, so as to keep one's mind free and at leisure.

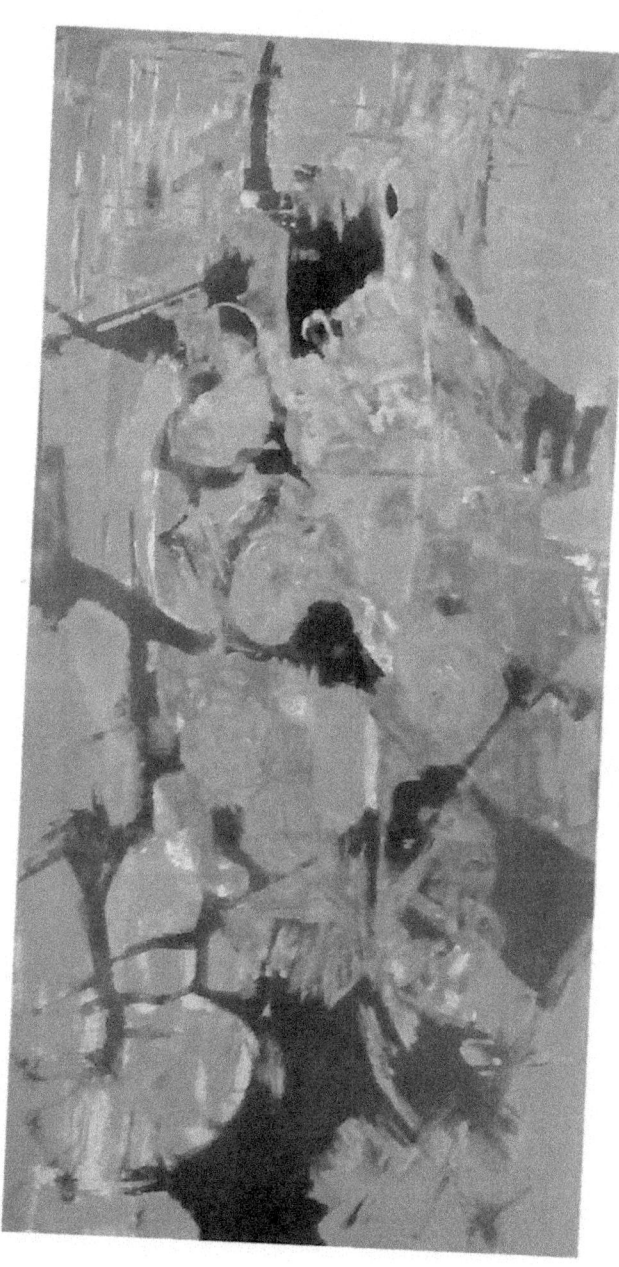

Tranh "Trừu tượng" (0,90x1m80) - 1967, sơn mài của họa sĩ Nguyễn Gia Trí
"Abstract" (0,90x1m80) - 1967, lacquer by artist Nguyễn Gia Trí

November 23, 1985

There must be an extremely great reason that instigates one to enter the desert.

The Masters didn't say much, little by little the sayings and teachings became numerous, due to people's talks.

Enlightened or not, one knows all by oneself, just like one knows one is drinking hot or cold water.

The canonical books are also the Buddha's icon.

Painting abstract means deleting all ancient rules, and going by contraries. While painting one is looking for ideas, and they materialize themselves in one's working process. A painting that is painted only after one has secured the ideas, is only an illustration.

The dexterities, if used too much, will become inefficient. It would be dangerous if one continues to use them. *"Mechanical work produces a mechanical mind"* as the old sprinkler in the Nan-Houaking.

The True Path is one, the various nations figure and

call it accordingly to the name adopted in each one of their countries.[1]

With the Roman Catholic religion, one wonders why God has sent his Son down to this world to be tortured and to die on the cross? These are problems that cudgel one's brains and cannot be solved.

With painting,the development of big rules are all similar to one another.

Language has many limits.

The main problem consists of developing "man". An "individual" without nationality, without occupation an

---

(1) According to Thavipuan, a Thai author, a hundred years ago, poet Tagore wrote about religion, to the effect that: "We have to get through that narrow borderline and support the whole India in striving for a good future. At that time, try to protect the right to have a holyday like previous ones. This "holy day" is a day that the Buddha's, the Christ's, and Mohammad's spirit gets mixed with one another".
It has been nine years now since 11th September 2001, the "holy day" mentioned by Tagore one hundred years ago becomes more pressing to the world. In my opinion, on that day, there must additionally be Confucius's, and Laotzu's spirit in that "mixture" hence "Five Great persons in one Way" or "five religions from the same (spiritual) source". Lasting world peace would start from that spirit, from the bloc of Asian countries, from all over the Asia. The Earth would be in peace for ever. "The glow of dawn will come from this horizon, in the East, where the sun rises", as foretold by the great poet Tagore.

unmixed man.[1]

Bumps, stumblings and difficulties are necessary for obtaining progress. If everything is favourable and smooth, there will be nothing new.

December 24, 1985

Art is like religion. One searches into one's source, looking for one's "initial form" ever since the time one's parents hadn't yet given birth to one, like patriarch Huệ Năng once said.

Like a dog, when chained up to the sutras, one isn't afraid of going astray.

Upon coming to one's senses, one feels afraid and deviated.

Only by loving Buddha, can one later enter religion and reach Buddhahood.

---

(1) Krisnamurti once said: every individual human equals the whole mankind; put him or her into any people would reduce his or her real dimension. In a UNESCO's magazine an African artist put it that: Modern art should aim at the clay human when made by God. The clay human and the Original face or Buddha-nature in Zen are the same.

It's good enough for one to remain natural. Of course, one has gone through the volitional gate. It's not suitable to overstrain and oblige oneself.

One's mind is immensely large. All elaborate scientific works come from it.

Buddha doesn't have wrong dreams.

One must have a profession that, later on, will become one's karma. That's why people use to say "nghề nghiệp" (profession and karma). Karma includes good one and bad one.

Look at everybody, and see neither good, nor bad.

There existed the story of two dogs that had gone astray in the North Pole and had to dig a hole inside a deep grotto to heat themselves. They had warmed themselves with their own heat. At times, dogs are much better than men.

True art has no time, no geography. It constantly lives its modern life. Picasso's words: *"Egyptian and Greek arts are ever modern"*, are also modern.[1]

The perturbing sounds in one's mind is also a ghostly thing.

See note on page 137.

Practicing religion means mending one's way.

The True Path has not yet been reached as one still has a least bit of doubt.

Working in lacquer, one doesn't regret money, time, as one is studying.

The sutras also suit each man, each time.

In the sutra, the term "kiến" (darshana) and "văn" (hearing) are often used as these terms are direct ones.

Practicing religion, and choosing an easy way, is like water flows into hollows. Favourable wind shies the dust, one should take a favourable condition to work.

Falling into a trance is a means to let the genius get hold of one's body. Some people become sick, because they're deeply infected with the beautiful voice and face of their falling into trance. Spiritualistic medium means togetherness.

---

(1) In a letter written in 1923, Picasso wrote: "To me there is no past or future in art. If a work of art cannot live always in the present it must not be considered at all. The art of the Greeks, of the Egyptians, of the great painters who lived in other times, is not an art of the past; perhaps it is more alive today than it ever was. Art does not evolve by itself, the ideas of people change and with them their mode of expression".

One's body, one 's hands and feet are all fakes.

One has to practice Endurance. Swallow everything. In life, women constantly dispose of us. While painting women, one must also swallow the aforesaid matter.

January 1, 1986

One must know the whole thing, in order to know the details. In all one's actions, one must conceive on a humanistic plane, so as to commit no mistake.[1]

---

(1) In the first year of the last century nineties, I had helped him to achieve the last work stages of a huge lacquer entitled "Centre of South and North springtime Garden"; at that time he had turned weak, and was needy, without any income from lacquer painting... at times, while stopping our work and resting, I had encouraged him: "Our country has been unified, maybe after we finish this painting, our Vietnamese people's heart will be unified both inland and abroad". He kept silent for a long moment, then simply said: "It'll be much more than that". The "Springtime Garden" painting, with poet Đào Duy Từ's two verses, written in Chinese and dealing with the flowers and the moon, that also constitute the painting's content, as he once said: "Only a benevolent heart can unify everybody". The name "Centre of South and North Springtime Garden" of the painting voices the artist yearning for a right place for Vietnam in the world and in the future. Since a long time I've heard about an oracle that has existed I don't know since when and that reads: "Vietnam is like a pagoda, for all nations in the world to come in and out during all four seasons". I also remember that the great former USSR poet Gamzatop once told a Vietnamese translator: "If we happen to have a new law code for the whole world, the brave Vietnamese deserve the right to write it's preamble..."

Nature is very large, it's limitless, unmistakable.

Sense-consciousness originates from the fact of coming in contact with one another, if one lives in the forest, one will not have sense-conciousness.

The True Path is something tasteless, a mouthful of pure water also has a flavour.

January 6, 1986

The stone slabs, cut off and polished constitute the image of idealistic lacquer substance.

We're only responsible for the living beings of our heart-of-hearts. Our heart-of-hearts has all kinds of living beings. Were we to transform all of them into Buddhas, then we have reached Buddhahood.

Working in lacquer means opening a new eye.

Divination is another world, not ours. It obstructs our reaching the one-pointedness of mind.

One studies, then teaches one's wife and children.

One must have a knowledge of the sea under many angles, at many times to throughly know the sea,

343

especially the storms, the tidal waves.

Everything that has become specialized is no good.

Being overcautious is also no good.

One does what the workmen cannot do. One has them worked with it, then one makes the correction. Use each man's capacity at the right place.

Bringing the True Path to life, without spoiling the ten thousand doctrines of the world, is quite difficult. Everything must be intact, harmonious, and developed.

When one is already accustomed to one's work, then one can go ahead to proceed, without having to calculate or be parsimonious.

Once we're "conscious", we even dare not to think of revenge, let alone taking revenge.[1]

June 4, 1986

When painting, between awakening and dreaming is a

See note on page 141.

sequence of continuous times. When dreaming, one always remembers when awakened. There are things no longer remembered, but they are still kept in one's deeper memory.

Working in a mechanical way engenders a mechanical mind.

June 22, 1986

Practicing religion means looking for "one's initial form". In a great majority of people, the distance for going back is dark and dense. Practicing religion, means easing and giving up that obstructing separation.

---

(1) When I asked him about the losses his family has had to suffer in wartime, he answered by this sentence. As when one practices religion, one practices it as a whole: "Body, Speech, Mental Conception". He also related that he had participated in the fight against the French, and as weapons and ammunitions were concealed in his workshop, and were found out by the French that arrested him, he was tortured by the French that wanted him to avow. Being not able to support the pains, he had hit his head three times on the ironwood floor to commit suicide. He added: "Later on they didn't torture or interrogate me anymore, and those French themselves had brought me a basket of boiled duck-eggs".
After 1954, when the country was divided, he was in the South and was once incarcerated in jail (I didn't ask him why). He said he had had to cut open his stomach trying to kill himself.
He said: When "we have gone our whole way" all things in the past must be overlooked.

The more one practices religion, the more one's body turns big. Like Buddha's body that is boundlessly large.

When not yet reincarnated, the ghost race is smaller than ordinary men, but they travel back and forth with lightning speed, and this period of time is called the Trung Ấm (Bardo or In-Between State in English). Ấm or Âm (Skandha) is a same word, pronounced differently.

The process of practicing religion and training oneself is the process of rearing the "Holy Foetus". Upon reaching the day, the month, one delivers it. When the midwife smacks one's bottom, one awakens.

Reading is useless,if one doesn't live a real life.

"Enlightenment" is like a sudden emotion, one is never able to forget.

"One shouldn't let one's mind be stuck and caught anywhere"[1] Don't let the religion-practicing-mind be stuck and caught anywhere.

The look of each person is different from the ones of the others. "Enlightenment" is at the centre, to be able to see it, one has to adjust one's eyes, from afar, near, big,

---

(1) A sentence in Vajracchedika Sutra.

and small just like adjusting a pair of binoculars.

The artist lives an eccentric life, compared with the one of a common person. People, as they are, remember while the artist forgets. The artist looks at things as a whole, people, as they are, look at details.

The artist produces to train and refines his presentiment. The heart can be trained. As for *"not being born, not being destroyed, not being formed, not being pure, not being increased, not being lessened"* [1], such states belong in the Buddha-Heart, Bodhi -Heart that are already perfected.

Presentiment is the state in which one knows and sees immediately, without having to analyze, calculate, or measure.

July 1986

The word "Hành" (Impression) aso means "Hạnh" (realized good wishes). With a monk, one doesn't say biography, but uses the term " hành trạng " (achievements). Sitting at one place while keeping on going, and not with one's feet.

---

(1) A sentence in Prajna Paramita Sutra.

"The effect and force" of lacquer is different from the one of oil paint, so the "hard pains involved" are also different from each other. Oil paint has no depth.

Standing beside the Angkor wat, one feels the telling verse of Bà Huyện Thanh Quan: "On the old way, the horse carriage seems like an ethereal soul. On the old base of the ancient palace, the sun is setling".

While reading Buddhist scriptures, the difficult thing is that one has to see them as a whole.

The Saddharmapundarikà-Sutra provides guidance for one to practice religion from Hinayàna to Mahàyàna.

Religious practice doesn't have inner or outer side. Saying one's prayers is like painting, one must be healthy and lucid, if one is sick but keeps on saying one's prayers, then this is intentional, mechanical.

Suchness means not similar to anything. Like a Buddha's follower: acting compassionately.

Understanding one's insight as penetrating the true essence of one's self isn't correct.

Painting doesn't need preference as one is after a higher preference. Painting doesn't need the Five

Aggregates as one is using something much higher. It's unconceivable, and one doesn't think, doesn't calculate, but remains silent.

Life turns round in circles. One must have the strengh to catapult oneself out of that orbit to gain freedom. One must catapult oneself many times.

In the occidental life, many people that looked for "freedom" have met with "libertinage". They don't understand that, when wishing to be free, one must know how to be self –restrained.

To be able to paint, one must conceive a passion for painting, and must weed out the daily concerns.

The abstract painting displays itself and brings forth shapes and patterns. It wouldn't be right, were one to have a previous idea to adopt.

Perhaps the "Vimalakirtinirdesha-Sutra" is the last one of all Buddhist scriptures.

The "Vimalakirtinirdesha" mentions that: language has its own form of liberation.

The Buddha's teachings reach his disciples, not through writings, but directly from mind-to-mind impartment.

The quicker one paints, the more one can learn everything from one thing.

One loses one's liberty because one takes heed to keep for oneself many things around one.[1]

Loathe all obligations. Have confidence that, as the days go by, one becomes better and better, as Buddha loathes no one.

Who can stop the falling leaf?

August 12, 1986

Glance off all figures. At first the painting might not have any distinct figure.

The brush stroke doesn't encompass the eggshell, but freely mingles with it and with the body.

Allow the paint or the lacquer to develop all its capacities.

If one pays much attention to details, one is

---

(1) Writer Henry Miller once said: At times one is drowned because... there are too many buoys.

weakening the whole painting. One must always pay attention to the painting as a whole.

Don't ponder, don't calculate, eggshell cracks naturally, like cracks on an ancient bowl, don't do anything that is not natural or spontaneous.

Illusion and reality are like lacquer and tracing-paper[1]. One must immediately see everything in a blink, time is the thing that obstructs that view.[2]

The religious that duly practices religion isn't bound by anything, and can be exempted from all means through a slightest manner.

One doesn't know yet whether one can arrive or not, but having a direction to follow is good enough.

The big and swift movements cannot be seen, what one can see are the small ones, the partial ones.

---

(1) Tracing-paper is used for sketching figures that will be transferred to the body for painting a lacquer.
(2) Bodhidharma has written:
"Bodhi has neither appearance,
Nor intermediary.
Neither shapes nor forms,
While pondering one loses one's means ...".

September 14, 1986

Once one has liberated oneself from a "hindrance", one can also escape from other "hindrances" easily.

"Hindrance" is a habit that is also called a cycle of existence.

Painting is to nourish, to offer, and when offering, one has to be respectful. In one's self, there is always something higher than oneself and this is different from the way the children play their worshipping game.

Life doesn't mean looking for leisureliness.

The most important thing is to look for the "one"[1]. Sadhana cannot be two. Depending on the level, people understand the "one" in various different ways.

The Buddha says only one word, while the living beings, depending on their levels, will understand in their own way, like each tree has its own flowers.

Time trains people to have endurance. If being not able to endure, one is like a dead person.

---

(1) One: A sole thought "Unique truth, alsolute truth (Patriarch Huệ Năng).

The primitive men living in grottoes also knew to make beautiful things. In daily life, each look insinuates various themes, like when cooking rice, one looks at the fire and sees the beauty of the fire...

A number of Picasso's paintings aren't true, as they don't represent his requirements. One must do whatever one wants to do.

On a painting, one has to work on important matters: materials, lay-out. As for the small things, they will work between themselves.

Adopting and practicing religion in the Smaller Vehicle school, one is adopting the *"poor doctrine"* that is quite narrow. Like someone suffering from a toothache and feels the pain as big as the Tu Di mountain. Practicing religion in the Great Vehicle school, one can easily go beyond all hindrances and difficulties.

Each man, each generation has his or its own works, no one can replace someone else.

September 20, 1986

One shouldn't analyze, instead, it's advisable to synthetize.

353

With a whole nation, whatever result it could reach, is thanks to its faith.

The land that produces diamonds is an repressed land.[1]

The work is precious because man has produced and made it precious, like a book is valuable because of the writer who wrote it. If not, it would simply be waste paper.

Some people say that practicing religion is aimed at putting to an end, once and for all, one's illusion. But, at times, illusion helps us to escape from many things.

_____

(1) In her whole history Vietnam exists next to the great country in the North (and was dominated by this giant for more than 1000 years), which always schemed to assimilated her for good at any cost. Every time they invaded our country, they strived to destroy all Vietnamese cultural achievement. With time, such adversity turned our feelings into a diamond-hard spirit of the perpetuated value in Vietnamese culture. It is also the source of our modern lacquered works. Searching the past, according to prof. Nguyễn Huệ Chi, we can see that, in "Việt Kiệu Thư", a Chinese book written in Ming dynasty in century XVI, Chinese historian Li Wen Feng reproduced the three decrees king Ming Chingtu had sent to Zhuneng, the Chinese commanding officer of the invading forces to Vietnam, of which a passage reads: "When having arrived in Annam (i.e. Vietnam), try to gather all their books including folksong books and children's songbooks, except those made by Chinese, and set them all on fire on the spot, a single piece of those stuff shall not be left. ALL STELAE IN THEIR COUNTRY, EXCEPT FOR THE ONES ERECTED BY CHINESE, MUST BE IMMEDIATELY SHATTERED RIGHT ON THE SPOT, NOT A PIECE OR A WORD OF THEM CAN BE LEFT INTACT".

Platon[1] is valuable because he conducts in-depth research works on man. The problem consists of throughly promoting man, causing him to reach Buddhahood.

Each artist has his own world. One would feel wobbly at the legs while rambling through one's frontiers, all the more paying attention to the ones of other people.

All working standards must have quickness as a criterion. All slowness and delay are unprofitable.

Beauty itself is the thing that records the trace of one's soul on the painting. Therefore, the development and the change of beauty originate from one's heart which constitutes a source.

At times, from technical things that have gone wrong spring up some new things. While improving the painting, one creates another beauty.

Zen experiences must be experimentative ones, one has to go through it to understand it, one just cannot simply talk about it.

The stroke is the "gist" of the figure,[2] so, whatever

---

(1) Greek philosopher (428-348 B.C).
(2) According to H.Reed, an art researcher, "The earliest artistic paintings ever appeared in history was those of cave dwellers. They started with lines depicting images. The art of painting started with line usage".

change might come with the mass of colours or the eggshell, one still can obstain distinguishable figures.

Perspective is effective only when the painting is small. With an extremely big painting, when taking a point to look at, one cannot see the painting as a whole, at only one time.

October 31, 1986

One must have one's inner strength, acquired through daily training, to be able to go across the time wall.

A big painting isn't an enlarged small one. The bigger the painting,the more inner strength is required.

No born, no slow, no quick. Time shall be transformed into space.

The artist's painting requires freshness, newness and sharpness.

At Gia Viễn, Nho Quan, Chi Nê (Ninh Bình), the mountains stand out like a Ha Long Bay on dried up land. The mountain lines are still sharp.[1]

---

(1) He might hint at the lines on a lacquered work when it has been sandground. Picasso also said, to the effect that, "A beautiful painting is one with bristling razors".

Painting or stopping, the painter or the painting is un-distinguishably inexistent.

Go, wait, and have confidence, and one will meet with (what one's expecting).

One must forget all that one has done to have new things. One must constantly rely on heavenly support.

One must reach the True Path through an unexpected Path. Like using a mirror to control, by means of letting the painting being reflected inversely on it. If the inverse image also looks correct, then the correctness is actually correct.

If time always goes clockwise, then there will be no dream at all.

Saying one's prayers is for detoxification. Practicing the buddhist doctrines without annihilating worldly doctrines.

December 6, 1986

It's thanks to religion that man is valuable. It's also thanks to religion that art is valuable.

The method of saying one's prayers is saying and remembering all prayers as a whole. At a certain moment, while meeting with some circumstances, one suddenly remembers.

Painting is for training one's eyes, training the look of one's mind, and the mistake consists of hoping for its result. Even when one isn't painting, one must also train one's mind. Practicing religion has no inner or outer sides, no means, "non-action and quietness".

The world's value resides in the Three Jewels: Buddha, Doctrine and Community of Bonzes, there is no other value besides them.

When wishing to go, one has to change and look for the suitable transportation means.[1] Flying into space, one uses balloon (filled with hydrogen gas), aircraft, missile etc...

How can one learns as there is nothing to know? How

---

(1) *Picasso once said: "No doubt, it is useful for an artist to know all the forms of art which have preceded or which accompany his own form. That is a sign of strength if it is a question of looking for a stimulus or recognizing mistakes he must avoid. But he must be very careful not to look for models. As soon as one artist takes another as model, he is lost. There is no other point of departure than reality".*

can one do as there is nothing to know? I'm as "blind" as you.

Working in collage is similar to construing one's horoscope, it's all the same, everyone is similar to the other.

The method for practicing religion has no inner or outer side. Practicing religion is like the illusion of ecstasy (Samadhi) as one sees no illusion at all.

When young one doesn't practice religion, it would be very difficult to do it when one becomes old.

January 6, 1987

Constantly keep in one's mind, in one's subconsciousness, the "instant" (Ksana-Ksanai). From time to time it would arise. The "instant" is also the "love" that cannot be eased, one is like someone having a lump in his throat.

Rendering services to the world, one's merit is never ended. Practicing religion in the Smaller Vehicle school is like placing a car on a platform and start the engine, permiting the wheels to run on the spot. It would spoil itself or would have no effect at all.

Ordinarily, when looking at a tree, one must see that it's a tree, if it turns into a snake, then it's awry already.

Working in lacquer takes quite a long time while one always feels that it's quick like painting Chinese ink painting. Strokes can be repainted,but still seem like being painted only once.

One must take the initiative with regard to all changes.

"Non-action and quietness", but it's also like "Action and unquietness", one seems to know all methods.

January 27, 1987

"Behave accordingly to the law".

The painting adapts itself to life, one must feel and consider oneself its relation with the public.

Once a method is adopted, one must follow it.

The creating artist is someone with a strong individuality. One's character is created by oneself.[1]

One must not be affected by the environment,as one's mind is left in another world.

---

(1) I asked him: "What if an artist doesn't have his own style?" He said: "So, that is nothing at all".

One must always lean on something to practice religion.

One's mind has many ways, many scenes to delude oneself.

Not spoiling the worldly laws means acting accordingly to customs, habits, and ethics of the world.

Everything that is genuine is hidden and doesn't reveal itself.

Understanding one's self is understanding one's body, character, soul, and directing it toward high- mindedness.

Each person has his own shape and individual character that can be read.

Everything must come from one's consciousness.

January 29, 1987

Genuine living cannot be explained, as it constantly changes. Were one to analyze it, it would be like dissecting a corpse, and it will no longer be right.

"Behave accordingly to the law" means acting accordingly to laws. One's life and work correspond to prayers.

361

Working in lacquer constitutes another living attitude, much better than working in oil paint.

The creating artist goes ahead, avoiding all reasoning and systems.

The universe is a big machine that cannot be seen and is called a great mystery.

While producing, it's not advisable to let the working time lengthened, as things will become flaccid.

The Hương (Perfume) pagoda would be nothing if it doesn't have a bonze, or the incense smoke of pilgrims, or if it happens not to be sacred.

To be able to achieved something, traditions and lineage are required. If one starts all by oneself, then it would be weak and fleeting.

One cannot take this one thing to measure the other thing, like using a clock's time to measure the one of one's soul.

Each "law" conforms to itself, like a man will give birth to a man, and not to a tree.

Everything springs from one's mind. An overturned mind would bring forth disordered actions.

The disadvantage comes from one's desire to change all the time.

March 5, 1987

The Vimalakirti sutra reads: "The mother is the Prajnaparamitas (penetration of mind leading to enlightenment) and the father is the Upàya (means)". The mother has more merits.

When one says that one is enlightened, while one actually isn't enlightened yet, one is like someone that is pregnant and that cuts off her placenta stem.

At first, it was only an illusion that was formed thanks to "dedication to the Buddha". If there is no "dedication", no respect, then nothing will be formed.

"The blest will have their shares of happiness". The word "phận" (fate) also means "phần" (share).

One doesn't paint with one's eyes, but with one's mind, and one is rational and idealistic.

"He who knows doesn't speak, he who speaks doesn't know" (Lao-Tzu). One ought to conceal this matter. If one mentions it clearly, concretely, at times, it's harmful.

The researcher, the writer, when having an individual view or something shifty, then genuine honesty it lost. The writer must use his prestige and even his own life to guarantee what he has written, in order to be useful to life. Like Bruno, Copernic, Galilée etc ...

The word "sinh" (giving birth) we are now using in the occidental sense means "sinh", giving birth to something. As for the word "sinh" in our own sense means "leaving" or "vãng sinh" (leaving this world for the land of Buddha).

The world manners distinguish male and female, but there is no distinction in the religious life.

One practices religion as one wishes to catch hold of "that leaving".

The revolutionist doesn't think of life or death. They summon up all their strength or even their lives to serve their cause. Once the success was achieved, the successors, if having no sense of responsibilities, can exploit that cause at their convenience.

March 24, 1987

Occidental philosophy limits itself within life, and still

cannot escape from death.[1]

Japan has all necessary means for lacquer painting, but it doesn't have a modern lacquer art, as means aren't the main thing.

March 25, 1987

The ant that crawls on the ground understands space differently from the mosquito that flies in space.

One must see the whole to understand the details.

Reading scientific books dealing with space is quite sluggish. One ought to blot it out once one has understood it. The professor of science, when explaining about space, has to use a piece of paper as an example, then has to twist it to show to his students. As for the artist, he twists space in his mind.

---

(1) *Zhuangzi said: "Only when having put the living aside will one thoroughly acquire his comprehension just in a moment. (Having thoroughly acquired comprehension just in a moment is to be enlightened in a sudden). Having been enlightened in a sudden one would be able to see the One. (Seeing the One - the Way). Having seen the One, one would no longer see the past and the present, and to enter the non-death and non-life region. Having killed the desire to live by oneself, one would not die. Living the life for oneself is not living".*

Buddha said: *"Only beauty is true"*.

Many people have gone to and fro the limit of life and death.

The man that enters the desert doesn't carry with him the icones.

The mosquito lives its existence and doesn't know that it's a mosquito. Only man knows all kinds of species.

There exist no orthodox and heretic, there are only good and evil. The main thing consists of not to do harm to life. Live outside of evil and good. Do not distinguish good and evil.

Man's life has flavours such as sweet, floury and buttery, bitter, salty and so on, but, finally, on second thoughts, there is actually only a unique flavour.

When being close to language, one is always bound.

"That matter of leaving this world" would be useless when talked about, were one to talk only for the sake of talking.

From one existence to another, one's heart is pierced without knowing how to cure it.

In this Jambudvipa continent, when still alive, people complain and bewail their lot. But upon leaving it, they begin to feel afraid.

March 29, 1987

The religious, when meeting with sufferings and afflictions, would remain unmoved. Only when being unmoved, can one see the truth. When an idea is bred, there is already a flaw and what one sees is no longer true.

The practice of Buddhist Zen is in favour of very little imagination. Seeing an uninitiated person, one doesn't hate, and seeing a saint, one doesn't love.

If one relies only on the aspect, then it would be too precarious. At my age, I don't rely on it anymore.

When practicing religion, one has to practice it as a whole and cannot practice it only partially. If one does so, one's practice will develop in a distorted manner.

When using illusion, one will be delusive.

The admirable art on the painting comes from the lacquer and isn't shown on the paint.

"Prajnaparamitas", "paramitas" also means the earth.

A big painting isn't an enlarged small one. It has its own rules.

Buddhism according to H.Miller[1] has been transformed.

One has to understand the universe to be able to understand the nation, the individual.

May 11, 1987

It's thanks to *"Contemplation"* [2] that life has been created.

"Mind" are numerous and change as fast as cloud and smoke. Only *"Contemplation"* is concentrated and formed. *"Mind"* is constantly in confusion and changing.

"Impression" (samskaras) cannot be seen. But *"Appearance"* has form and aspect, constantly leaving traces.

"Achievements" constantly need new thing and change.

---

(1) American writer.
(2) The mind observes and concentrates on a scene (matter of reason) without disunion or tremendousness. (Dictionary of Buddhism by Đoàn Trung Còn).

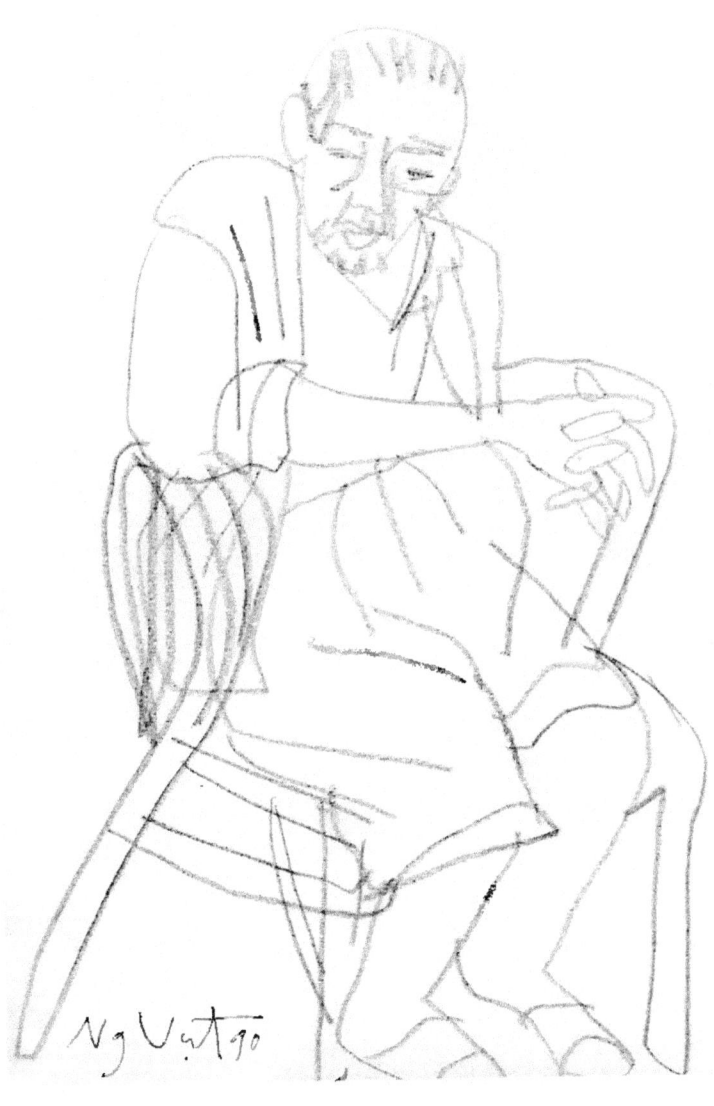

"Họa sĩ Nguyễn Gia Trí trong xưởng vẽ" ký họa của Nguyễn Xuân Việt
"Artist Nguyễn Gia Trí inside his studio" sketch by artist Nguyễn Xuân Việt

It's the residues of life that engender the thoughts. Man's mind is a heap of residues.

In painting there exist also quite a great deal of residues.

The oil painter is not allowed to enjoy the time of the painter working in lacquer.

Looking at a painting means looking at the heart, the liver, the lung and the gut of the painter, and this is the most appropriate way to look.

The painting is the thing one creates oneself. If one is bound by it, then one is being materialized.

The narrow ideas of the Smaller Vehicle practician always have residues.

A lacquer is never terminated. Anyone of the lacquers is a sketch.

The artist even retains the rough strokes, the spoiled ones and the mistakes in a natural manner.

I dream of painting a long stroke, as thin as painting with a ball-point pen on the lacquer.

The artist can easily be subject to rules like a train travelling on a railway.

The *"Contemplation"* while producing is a temporary one.

June 10, 1987

One forgets whatever one has done, and no "law" will be established.

One produces the painting, then one oneself doesn't understand it, and this is something actually true.

Painting a work as small as a stamp,or as big as the Tu Di mountain, while feeling as if one weren't painting anything, means one's actually "enlightened". This is because everything will be lost, destroyed.

Each man's age is different from the ones of other people. At times, the son's age is older than the one of the father. And this is question of the age of training and studying through many past lives.

It's not easy to have a karma. One acts as a painter in order to strike out one's karma.

The trace on a painting is easy to blot out. A trace in one's heart is difficult to remove, and that's the reason why metempsychosis does exist.

When painting with an aim or an intention, the result would be not very good. One ought to paint while playing and meditating at the same time.Just like studying and playing at the same time to acquire some knowledge is different from studying to attend an examination, these two ways of studying are quite different from each other.[1]

"One's "mind" is like the sound wind,
One's "temperament" is as light as fleawort.
Don't ask about death and life, evil spirit and Buddha,
Thousands of stars head towards the North, while waters flow towards the East".

Tuệ Trung Thượng Sĩ

There exist planets on which, one springs only one step to reach one hundred metres high. All rules on weight and all other rules in each planet are different from the ones in other planets.

---

(1) There are some earthly advantageous studies as mentioned by a German philosopher: A number of people learn too much. They are like vultures flying very high in order to see clearly some carcasses on the ground.

There are various kinds of scales: scales for weighing gold, scales for weighing fire-wood, and scales for weighing rice. Horoscopy is only a child's play.

Penetrating everything like penetrating everybody. Everything is like the moon at the water bottom.

"Illusions" are things one cannot catch hold of.

There is no question as well as there is no answer. The question is also the actual answer.

The question of the Trần dynasty practicing Religion is not different from the question of the Trần dynasty fighting against foreign invasion.[1] When Trần Hưng Đạo was about to pass away, the king asked him what should be done to ward off the enemy? Trần Hưng Đạo answered: *"If they come in a reconciling manner, we must be very careful, but if they swoop down on us, there is nothing fearful"*.

The cycle of death and rebirth is like satellites being attracted by the earth. One must have a strong pushing force, so as to slide out of it.

One shouldn't say *"Knowing nothing is also having nothing"* when one is not in such or such situation.

───────────

See note on page 169.

Were one to follow and imitate a saint, one wouldn't succeed.

Painting landscapes is similar to painting people, eggshell, lacquer, all disappear, all change.

Finally, one also comes back to the question of "to be" or "not to be". What's "to be"? And "What's not to be"? Just like "hungry", "no longer hungry", when one is "hungry", when one is "no longer hungry"?

Wanting to paint some more doesn't depend on me.

---

(1) I gave him the book "Trúc Lâm Tông chỉ nguyên thanh", a work by Ngô Thời Nhậm. In the book there is this passage: "Seeing the Purusa-damya-sarathi (one that has brought people's passions under control, that is, King Trần Nhân Tông) coming to live at Hoa Yên Pagoda, people said that he got Pravraj (leaving home to become a monk). We know that he considered the people and country the most important. The country was in peace but his mind could not be at rest as he did not feel secure when thinking about the big neighbour in the North. That worry could not be mentioned obviously, as it could cause people's restlessness. He chose to have a pagoda built on Mount Yên Tử, the highest mountain, from there one could look as far as to Yên Quảng in the East, and to the two Lạng provinces in the North, in order to guard the safety of the country. He was like a Mahasthama-prapta Bodhisattva". (rendered from Vietnamese translation by Cao Xuân Huy).
I asked him why the king, who had become a monk, continued worrying about the safety of the country? He did not answer. Only when having grown up did I learn that the religion could become guiding light when it was in the heart of a free people.

One suffers the greatest tie,when one ties up oneself.

The character temperament is represented by the character heart placed beside the character life.

If there is neither interior, not exterior, where can the water leak and flow?

June 29, 1987

The True Path is like a rainbow, upon approaching to catch hold of it, it disappears.

All methods, after being achieved, must be discarded.

Working in "form" and "substance" is very difficult. Swimming in water is easy, but swimming in wood and stone is completely different.

Scriptures guide the artist in his work.

Once one has dived under the water, even the moonlit night no longer has the moon. The moonlight reflected on the water is also deformed. It's not important because of the deep water, but it's important because of the diver.

"The law cannot be humorously talked about", one cannot squabble about the law.

The main thing is that one must have *"faith"*. But *"faith"* when reasoned about has become *"superstition"*.

"The sight", one can naturally enjoy it and "see". As for reasoning, reading, saying prayers, all such matters may result in one "seeing nothing".

One has to practice religion in order to be able to explain the canonical books.

One's mind is like a sheet of white paper, which is lost when cut off, or even a needle point can leave a trave on it, more especially as it cannot be seen.

The Buddhist calendar uses the day the Buddha passed away to start a year. The Buddha passes away also means He is born.

Cleanse one's body and soul, then "It" is there already.

There is no Smaller Vehicle or Great Vehicle. The smaller practician will become small and the greater practician will become great.[1]

---

(1) Greek poet Yannis Ritsos wrote: "The real man stature is always measured with the dimension of freedom".

July 30, 1987

"Human heart is like sheets of paper, each one of them is thin i.e mean.
Worldly affairs are like chess games, each one of them is new".

With a painting, the important moment is the one in which one is working. Once achieved, whatever its fate might be, so much the worse for it.

Buddhist psychology is complete and thorough, factors which occidental philosophy fails to have. Once one has read the Vimalakirti, one'll see that there is nothing one can do.

Merits are in one's heart, only the doer knows about them, things that could be seen are only partial.

Buddhism has a great deal of sutras, but there are only a few that are the main ones, as for the remaining ones, they're numerous because they have been reasoned out by people.

It takes quite a long time to have someone that can achieve something new.

August 7, 1987

While producing, one doesn't know where one is. Everything constantly flows away.

Like a poem, one has to achieve the abstract painting before naming it.

The artist and the materials mingle into one, and this also applies to literary writings. There must be someone that selects, one has emotions as one has selected.

While creating, all rules and statutes are harmful.

Question: For what purpose does the artist produce?
Answer: Looking for liberty.

The surface of the painting might be uneven and bumpy.

Young people often sin against modesty and are frivolous, as they don't know things as a whole. Their knowledge are often borrowed ones.

Everything produced by the five senses are false.

What one does is the thing that cannot be seen and "unthinkable".

One produces one hundred paintings to choose only one. At times, one throws away all of them, or among one hundred, one gets only a half of one of them.

Lacquer painting is difficult as lacquer has many layers. As for the other types, it suffices to smear the surface, therefore, they are heterogenous.

The artist stands out and keeps silent, with neither profit nor harm.

One uses the sharpness for oneself, to reflect on oneself.

One has to work with an interrupted length of time for the *"liveliness"* to come.

When wishing to purge one has to enter the desert.

With certain painting one feels that it's "good" as one's five senses communicate with one another.

Creating means working at something that *"cannot be seen"*, therefore, there is no room for criticism.

Have a pure and calm look.

The Occidentals are sharp-minded with regard to one

thing. The Orientals are sharp-minded with regard to another thing.

The Asians say *"belly"* as they use this term to designate their mind, and as they don't want to use the term *"mind"*, and also use the term *"belly"* as a central part.

August 17, 1987

With art, the main thing is whether one dares to go to extreme limit or not?

Studying means constantly working on new things.

What excites the admiration is one's mind. As for one's product, it's only a false thing.

Conducting research works on colours is at times already old-fashioned.

Entering the desert (living aloof) so as to acquire a brand-new mind.

From the atomic bomb to all kinds of machineries, all such things are created by man's mind.

Toward where civilization has been heading in these last twenty centuries? It's always a vicious circle.

Art inherits the ancient things, and also inherits the sufferings.

Village temple sculpture belongs in the beyond compare type. The slashes, chiselling so easily into hard wood, are like when one is peeling a sweet potato. One seems like chiselling for fun, without feeling any tiredness. It's similar to European Gothic art.

Reading the Vimalakirti, one sees that everything can be possible, but everything can also be not possible. From raising one's foot to placing one's foot, both actions are carried out within the religious land (Bodhimandala).

Liberation is known only by the one that liberates himself. There exist many ways. One shouldn't use one's limited knowledge to measure everything. Man's life is short, one should use it in a most valuable way.

While writing, Kim Dung is like a Master illusionist. Balzac fell sick after writing his novel "Eugénie Grandet". They live with their personages.

One knows the new because one has distinguished.

One must renounce everything to have something new.

Let's take an example: in art, when creating

something new and we happen to be behind the times, then it'll be like other people are making the *"atomic bomb"* while we're making *"bows and swords"*.

One can imitate one hundred persons without being similar to any of them. *"Absorbency of people's essence"*.

Falseness is harmful to the student.

The Bodhisattvas that appear as Devils (Maras) can be seen only by people that are highly initiated.

Only by acting contrarily to art, can one understand art.

September 7, 1987

The thing one has known before isn't one's real knowledge.

Use the unique and everything will be right. "Unique truth, absolute truth".

One doubts when there are several instead of only one. When doubting, one creates a stain and pureness is lost.

Creating is forgetting, it's because one remembers, that one returns to the old spot.

Only by stating a question in a clear manner, can one solve the same question in a clear manner.

Why don't we paint directly? Paint without model, without needing documents. We paint accordingly to whatever we want, without needing to resemble anything.

Upon showing one's anxiety, one has gone out of the matter. There must be two when one compares.

Man is an anxious animal that is like a tangled thread. There are always two matters such as Yin and Yang.

Getting to a place one cannot think or discuss. An unconceivable place in which one cannot clutch or compare.

Starting to produce a painting is starting a game. But all games must come to an end. Paint, while seeming as one doesn't paint anything. One doesn't paint, while seeming as one always paints.

Paying too much attention to minor things, to details, is harmful.

It wouldn't be good were one to be vague while painting.

If most of one's feelings are for "*the One*", then the

remaining feelings are lessened.

Taoism and Buddhism are close to each other, as they both have the same source: HEART (Hridaya).

When one dreams, the dream is genuine, as for the dream depicted, it isn't a real dream.

October 6, 1987

The painter paints to seek liberty. It would be good if day after day, he's feeling freer and freer.[1]

Oil paint is easy to manipulate, therefore it flows straight, and doesn't have much effects on the painter.

We have the word "hủ" (antiquated), after a long time, the soya bean turns into salty soya marmalade. Only "voidness" can preserve itself from being antiquated.

The teacher, when wishing to explain to his students,

---

(1) Once I visited artist Bùi Xuân Phái, on whose desk there was a sheaf of reproductions of Picasso's paintings. He said: "Picasso's paintings are freer than mine".
When I showed Nguyễn Gia Trí, at his studio, two small abstract paintings of mine, pointing at one of them he said, "This one is freer than the other".

must gather his ideas together. Each meeting is a time for one to talk about new things that have never existed, among which there is a thing that will never be talked about for a second time, while there are also things that are' repeated over and over again. Certain thing has been mentioned and has turned blurred, leaving no active trace in the students.

November 26, 1987

Compassionate mother, stern father.

Voidness. Excellent possessions. There exists false "voidness".

With lacquer, it's very difficult to produce brisk strokes. Pay attention to the movement, right at the beginning.

Stroke with eggshell is also brisk.

Chagall paints, leaving the canvas on the table, and doesn't move away from it.

Question: Why at the time, right after the liberation, the sceneries in the South are different from the ones in the North, but at the present time, they are quite alike?
Answer: Before the sceneries in the South are different from the ones in the North, because people's heart and mind were divided. Now, they look alike as "people's heart and mind are all in one piece".

Painting for three or four years, is like painting for five minutes.

"Geography": The *"Earth"* has its *"reason"*, that remains unknown [1].

The main thing consists of solving the relation between people and people.

"Thọ" means "Receive" as well as "Thụ". "Thọ mạng" (Longlife) means receiving one's "mạng" (life). Previously it was always "none", it's because one has received, that it becomes "existing" [2].

Practicing religion, one constantly has to lean on something. One leans on the Four Blessings: the Moon, the Sun, father, mother etc ...

---

(1)The cultural and traditional geography of Vietnam is a "midway" position between two biggest cultural strands of humankind i.e.India and China. The marriage of the Vietnamese culture with the Occidental cultures toward the middle of the recent 19th century, through the French culture, has provided the modern cultural achievements of Vietnam with much value, particularly the creation of the method of using lacquer in modern art: "The synthesis of the Ocident and the Orient, basic to the pureness of mankind, constitutes a question of life and death, and might be the most urgent problem of our era". G.M.Herzen.
(2) A Zen master on Mount Tà Lơn wrote: "The nature that one discerns by himself is the highest; the life given by one's teacher is the greatest".

385

Buddhism contains everything.

All the troubles reside in the fact that one always want to obtain "Completeness" (Nita Artha), with something that's square, one wants it to be round, and what's it for?

December 29, 1987

"When illuminated through facts, wherever one goes, one is not afraid of losing one's thought (snoti). When illuminated through books, one's strength is weak". Bodhidharma.

While saying one's prayers, one must have impression (Samskaras) and meditation, in order to be able to understand.

Working on art doesn't mean producing something to hang on the wall.

One's body is "false", everything else is "false". Being "seemingly true" is already quite difficult.

I've gone to and fro, and have been close to death several times, so now I'm fed up with it upon seeing it.
"Being unwise means having nothing?"

The main thing still resides in one's true intention. One

isn't subject to material transformation.

Everything resides in oneself. If something is not useful for oneself, it will not be useful to anyone else.

When one's heart is sick, one's body is also sick.

Anything that is deep,cannot be spoken of.

There are things that at first were only a "fashion", but if they fail to develop, then they are only like soap-bubbles.

Don't let anything dusty.

Pre-war poetry is a part of French poetry that has been made Vietnamese. French poetry originates from Greek and Latin poetries.[1]

---

(1) He added: Xuân Diêu or Huy Cận has had a verse describing a girl's feet to the effect that the feet were as round as piles. If the reader was a European, he would imagine the marble white, whereas Vietnamese readers would think of the columns of a communal house. That is a spot in initial poems of our New Poetry.

That a lot of pre-war artists and men of letter made their appearance marked the time in which modern Vietnamese individuals affected by French culture and European free ideas rose to create. It was really a cultural revolution under the colonialist and feudal regime. (Chinese writer Lu Xun said: in the feudal regime there were only mandarins and common people). It is especial with poetry that Chế Lan Viên had his first work "Điêu Tàn" (Falling into ruins) published when he was just 16 years old; at the age of 21 Huy Cận had his "Lửa thiêng" (Sacred fire) published. With Xuân Diệu, Hàn Mặc Tử, Nguyễn Bính, they were the cream of the people, the new genius of a thousand years of Vietnamese poetry.

Jesus was crucified when he was only a little over 30 years old.

Character has no shape.

Character can be seen in a clear heart.

All the icons of various religions are different from one another, this is because the heart's shape had been seen.

Being illuminee means illuminating oneself. Each tree blooms its own flowers.

March 17, 1988

Understanding that one is *"laying down one's heart for giving alms"*, means that one is working on painting and producing beauty for everybody, is a very rudimentary way of understanding. Each species sees beauty in its own way.[1]

A painting, when achieved, is like one has brought the Tu Di mountain and all species into a grain of mustard, while the Tu Di mountain continues to be hugely big and the species continue to live, without knowing anything.

"Unmindfulness" is the biggest *"Void"*.
"Nobles and common people are on an equal footing".

One can be a high official, one can be a human manure collector, there is no difference or separation.

Artists that compete with one another for wealth and glory are no good. The thing for comparing is something else.

When one has nothing different with everybody, then there is nothing to say. If one happens to say something, that's for other people to understand.

Sorrows bring about the thus-come Buddha. On muddy land blooms the lotus. Seeds sown on a high mountain would not grow.

Every religion nurtures a womb (a holy womb). Buddha also does so.

A woman at her last moment has two words: chastity and obedience. I'm like a woman.

If one only meditates confusedly, aimlessly, then one is like a car one has started the machine and left there.

"*Far and near are free, nobles and common people are on an equal footing*"[1] there is neither far nor near,

---

(1) *A pair of parallel sentences at the Quán Sứ (Great Buddha) pagoda in Hanoi.*

neither near nor distant relationship, everybody is one.

With character and form mingled into one, one has the "truth".

Time causes everything to become "one".

The Saddharma-pundarika-sutra reads: *"Buddha is like a rich father, ordering his son to be brought back"*. The Maitreya-sutra reads: *"There are always thousands of Maitreya Buddhas that preach sermons, but no one listen to them!"*

Looking with mortal's eyes means looking with blind eyes.

When Buddha says tearing one's parents' eyes out, he's saying it in a figurative sense, and this means changing the look of one's parents by means of another eye.

One lives exactly in the same way with the way one performs art. Gold eggshell and earth powder have a same value.

"An eminent person would meet with some high-minded man that holds sway over him".

Everything and all creatures are created by one's heart.

Question: How should one go to the Buddha for refuge?
Answer: Go to the master that understands one's feeling best, that already knows, even when one hasn't thought of, or spoken yet.

One remembers somewhere the ages of layers of paint.

The Viên Giác (Complete Enlightenment) sutra reads: "While practicing religion, if one fails with a doctrine, one can adopt another one".

April 16, 1988

While studying, working, living, one ought to ignore all outside formalities.

In Kim Dung's cloak and dagger novels, the language used has developed and reached mysticism and marvelousness.

Performing art, one must act so as to see no law, no intention, such as wanting something to be hard, to be strong etc...

For one, the lacquer is like a friend, a wife, and the paint is actually oneself. One must see its character, and must know what it feels, what it wants.

Performing art, one must see to it that one's thoughts

391

penetrate inside all the materials one's using.

Like an animal swimming in water that flows swiftly, and that animal went by without leaving any trace.

Saying prayers gives us energy just like drinking water and eating one's meal, and then, one constantly has new strength.

Reading English is for meditating about its inner side, its contents. Studying the foreign language means studying its spiritual value.

Painting is like eating one's meal: "Three bowls of rice a meal and three suits of clothes" (strick necessities), it would be unprofitable to eat too much.

Upon producing, one ought to think of a way to solve the question in an easy manner.

Paintings cannot be classified and divided: art painting or painting for earning one's living, everything cannot be two and must be one.

Being able to do like Âu Dương Phong[1], one might be strong, but would give birth only to monstrosities.

---

(1) A character in a Chinyong's romance.

The religious from the smaller vehicle school, going into the desert all alone, is somewhat anti-natural, as all species that heaven and earth have given birth to, have had couples.

The earthworm is also a Buddha's teaching.

April 18, 1988

One paints abstract because there are too many intentions, and each one of them always wants to be present.

One's heart also has its king that arranges and harmonizes everything. When wishing to arrange and harmonize one's intentions, one must have one's "foregoing mind".

Peoples in the past worshiped time, people from each country have their own way of recording the traces. China transcribed history. Egypt built the Pyramids. Actually time doesn't exist.

The ant has its own universe. The elephant has its space. Man, while walking, sees space opening behind his step. The infirm sees space by means of looking at other people with a different look.

The metaphor one can use for ever is *"the finger*

pointing at the moon".

One must have strength to be able to work. Strength is given by Buddha. One must have a big vow to be able to achieve great things.

There is no distance between oneself and other people.

In one's studies, the essential consists of *"seeing the key problems"*, otherwise, however big and long studies one's achieved, they'll lead to nowhere.

To be an expert on a language is fairly difficult already.

Sorrows are Buddha's seeds.

The word "Cư" (Buddhist layman) also exists in Buddhism: "Tịnh cư" (living quietly) [1]

Language ties, language is also deliverance. Ties involve sorrows and happiness. Both factors tie up people.

---

[1] *Painter Nguyễn Gia Trí related: in his childhood he was a very feeble little boy, being afraid that he might die, his parents named him Nguyễn Gia Cư (Nguyễn, dwelling in his family) ; later on, an association called "Khai Trí Tiến Đức" (Association for the Intellectual Formation of the Annamese) was founded in Hanoi, his parents changed his name that becomes Trí.*

Working in lacquer, one carries out difficult principles, then forgets about them.

June 22, 1988

Practicing religion means *"concentrating"*. Breaking up means diluting. While concentrating, one's mind turns dense, and one's creative capacity develops.

Superhuman strength and liveliness means capacity reaching a high level. One could be disturbed if painting also oil paint.

In life, painting and Sutras have a close relation.

Painting means learning to forget, remembering is man's natural habit.

There exist many types of desires (Kãma). Buddha said parting from desire, and didn't say extinguishing desire, as after one extinguishes a desire, it'll transform itself into another one.

When attracted by many aims, one loses one's liberty and is far from one's main objective.

Sketching is a means to retain one's initial intention, not permitting it to be changed.

The thought appears on the painting, as for the creative capacity, it remains intact.

If Zen only means sitting still, then the orangutans have become Buddha since time immemorial. While sitting in meditation, one doesn't see anything.

To liberate oneself from the master's presence, one has to see the master's weakness.

Beauty has no competition and comparison.

One is easily misled and is often satisfied with one's achievements.

Reading English, and understanding dimly, causes one to be bound and confused.

Worshipping must involve faith to have effects on one's mind.

One ought to compare one's painting with nature.

While producing, were one to feel no emotion and pleasure, one has painted mechanically.

Laying out means arranging rationally.

July 19,1988

Talent is quite fleeting. Practicing religion is also transitory. Like in man's life, it suffices that an artery, as small as a hair, is blocked in one's heart to cause one to faint.

One has to practice religion in a sound way to be able to develop. It's the same with painting.

Painting means practicing to move one's hands and feet without thinking about anything.

There must be clashes, and chafings to engender "*voidness*". There's nothing. Empty language.

Simply because one's penetrating the truth, and there is nothing else to be discussed about.

It's one's working that produces the painting and clearly does everything.[1]

Talent and religious practice, one can have them without efforts.

----

(1) Picasso: "When I am dreaming, I do not see anything out of the ordinary. It is the outcome of work which makes the greatest contribution to creation. If we never arrive at this astonishment about our work, we never create new forms". (Souchère, 1960, page 15).

Once married, one has to double one's efforts. Practice forbearance, from one forbearance will spring up other ones.

August 13, 1988

"Like man, like dream". Beauty doesn't resemble one exactly.

One cannot forget an in-depth dream.

Big paintings involve many easier elements.

There are failures one has to proceed along with them.

One has an abstract hole in one's head.

Once one has applied the "Thy will be done" as a form and habit, then there will be no more effect.

One has a sense of working which seems like non-existent.

August 14, 1988

There exist the shining and the dim forms. No scratches. If there is a scratch, it has to follow the contour of the figure.

Paying attention to the whole more than paying attention to details.

Painting with eggshell means the eggshells paint themselves, one's hand cannot paint.

September 16, 1988

Have plasticity.

Once the lacquer is achieved, the lacquer substance shows up like something *"divinely shaped"*.

In lacquer painting, inside the extremely big exists the extremely small. While in the extremely small, one sees the extremely big. It's something no other substance can have.

While working on the details, constantly pay attention to the whole.

One has to take risks.

The dark and light changes of eggshell must be harmonious. The transparency of silver and gold must be mixed with the muddiness of powder.

October 1, 1988

Reading too much books and newspapers causes one's mind to turn dilute.

Upper, lower and all around, one's mind cannot fasten on to any place.

One cannot catch hold of everything around oneself, it's as slippery as an eel. One must have something firm to lean on.

The reason for which one commits failures is that one hasn't yet reached thoroughness.

There's a law above all laws.

It's best to make progress in lacquer technique, not for any purpose.

October 30, 1988

All excellent spots are obtained by chance. It's thanks to matters of mere chance that one doesn't turn mechanized.

Polish naturally to obtain smoothness. Fill in and patch places that are broken.

400

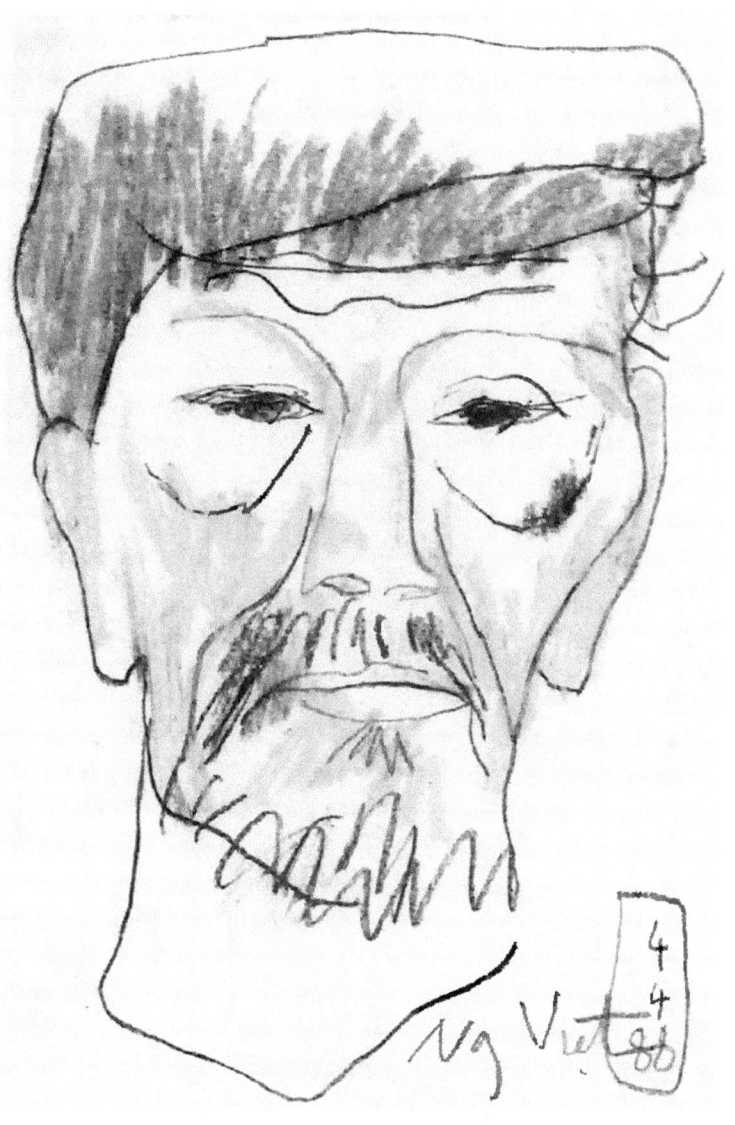

Tranh "Chân dung họa sĩ Nguyễn Sáng" ký họa của Nguyễn Xuân Việt
"Portrait of artist Nguyễn Sáng" sketch of artist Nguyễn Xuân Việt

Paint first, argue later.

While arguing one has become two.

In this modern time, everything runs in a race with time. As for lacquer it works exactly by contraries.

All constraints are due to one constraining oneself. Even the constraints cannot constrain one.

November 4, 1988

A beautiful handwriting isn't the ordinary beauty. At times, an unsightly handwriting is beautiful, as it has individuality and liveliness.

At times, one modifies the pen to suit the way of writing. The pen one uses can follow one. But, it isn't suitable for one to follow it.

The Nôm (demotic characters) has its own creativeness.

November 13, 1988

The secret of art consists of never doing anything intentionally.

Leave the dimness, maintain the shine. Oil paint is different from lacquer because it has no lustre.

November 19, 1988

One knows how one is. Whatever praise or blame cannot have any influence.

Keep silent and give such things a wide berth.

November 25, 1988

One has to go through failure to reach success. At a flushing level.

Go ahead and venture, provided that smoothness is obtained.

Avoid taking great pains to do the work.

Don't work intentionally at any particular spot, all spots are on an equal footing.

Painting, working freely without paying attention to scheduled time.

December 5, 1988

Producing is like taking a walk near a water well. One can do whatever one wants. Now, one has no time to take a walk.

A big painting is like a piece of soap, one can carve anything on it.[1]

In the working process, all fortuitousness can be widely developed into new beauties.

December 30, 1988

Polish, polish and in the long run it'll be finished.

Something vaguely spoken will engender something that's not vague at all.

One has to be more selective. One cannot select, as it's something that cannot be selected.

Be simple, with too many strokes, people would say one's finical.

---

(1) He refers to the work entitled "Centre of South and North Spring Garden".

Art means having *"Great confidence"*. I daren't speak out, being afraid I might be blamed by other people.

Beauty is constantly a great attraction from the big *"void"*.

Liveliness has neither inner nor outer.

A lacquer must be left for a long time to permeate.

There exists a painting one has tried one's best to repair it, but in vain. Later on, it could repair itself.

While working, one's heart must be pure so as to be able to avoid all deviation due to illusion. There exist thousands of illusions, while there is only one truth.

When painting quickly, one has to do so since the beginning. Just like when being free, one must be free since the beginning.

While paying too much attention to carry out what one desires, one might spoil it.

Only China is the land proper for the development of Buddhism.[1]

See note on page 201.

January 13, 1989

On the painting, one must know how to support the unsightliness. To be harmonious, a painting must contain both beauty and unsightliness.

There are spots one intentionally makes them unsightly and awkward for the sake of naturalness.

While shining the lacquer, one chafes regularly, then at a certain moment everything turns dazzling.

The shining rate must be average.

While shining, chafe the lacquer as a whole. Don't distinguish or pay particular attention on any spot. Everything must be on an equal footing.

---

(1) Maybe the first time he had read a Buddhist Sutra is in China. He related: before 1945, he paid a visit to a pagoda on a mountain in China with a friend. He liked the pagoda scenery very much and told the head bonze: "The scenery is so beautiful, suppose I were to live here forever". The Chinese head bonze said: "You'll have to go down there to pay your debt, there's no way you can live here". Upon leaving, the head bonze of the monastery told him: "Your friend is an easy speaker and is intelligent. As for you, you're slow and true-hearted, I wish to offer you this Diamond Sutra".

Question: Why a researcher once said that: "Lao-Ji's Taoism is a "life defending philosophy?".[1]
Answer: Taoism is for one to live, not to die.

The "permanence" that's synonymous with eternity isn't the common ordinary.

Language is a hindrance as it's disrupting.

Question: When the strokes, figures and colours of an abstract painting are correct?
Answer: When everything is reduced to silence.

The younger the painter is,the more unexpected changes are involved.

Working in lacquer and realizing great and labored paintings, one has to retire within oneself very much to be able to achieve them, and has to act as if one were dead.

Practicing religion cannot be defined. Upon saying that one's practicing religion, one actually doesn't do so.

A painting is something that's real close to the heart's essence.

_____

(1) With Lao-Ji, painter Nguyễn Gia Trí once said: "He is the most intelligent Saint among the Saints".

Devils also like to bully like men, one must retire within oneself to have a firm spirit.

While creating, at times, one doesn't know what to do and is completely blind.

Classical plastic art and folk images always send out new things.

Upon saying that one is loving until one turns blind, one's speaking in a figurative sense.

The fact that a lacquer takes a long time to be achieved, is due to the requirements of techniques.

Paying too much attention to minor things and details causes one to forget the main thing. Giving too much of one's attention to too many things, causes one to have a dilute mind.

The following painting step must not be contrary to the previous one. One has to work continually.

March 3, 1989

Painting means looking for the fright to master it.

Work in such a way as not to take too much great pains.

One must commit failures to have things to mend.

What is unintentional but is successful is quite good.

When first painted, the painting looks small, but later, it looks larger and larger.

A piece of wood, or a piece of hard iron, twisting and swirling in one's meditation, would create a quite different space.

"It" isn't a science, and also isn't a philosophy. Music causes calmness to be lost. Without calmness, one just cannot meditate.

Music also exists in painting. None of the figures remains still.

One can insert the eggshells horizontally, vertically, backwards and forwards, as one wishes.

Intelligence solves all matters.

"Practicing religion", one is like a "dead and buried" person.

It's not true that natural is always good.

Some substance is blemished or dim all by itself. But

the lay-out has to be the promotor. At times, it might be changed entirely.

With some persons, their paintings assume an air of difficulty, very hard to realized.

The *"Emptiness"* (space) has many different *"compartments"*.

The Occident is inclined towards matter, although it understands that it isn't the substance of things.

A painting achieved at a stretch isn't as good as the one achieved little by little. As in this latter way, it's closer to the development of life.

Go ahead and start from a real matter, then it'll become surrealistic. And originating from something "surrealistic", it will become the common real matter [1].

Train the eggshell, from a hard matter, to become something supple.

There is no fortuitousness. Here, fortuitousness means

---

(1) *There is a saying in an Indian ancient story that goes: "Starting from something real, one has both real and unreal, while starting from something unreal, one has neither unreal nor real".*

a stop in a blink of the hard and painful process.

Intelligent and fast is harmful.

To know whether it's smooth or not, one has to shine and compare it with the whole area.

Strokes and masses are intermingled, one has to adjust the high and low parts. Were one to overlay, the painting will turn blurred.

Masses, colour streaks must also breathe, one has to make them spongy.

March 17, 1989

Poetry is music, literature also needs music.

Picasso 's painting is cold and has a little music.

Lacquer needs large sizes, it befits religious themes, like Chagall's paintings.

Only things one can do oneself are lasting.

Large paintings need extremely beautiful sketches.

It's really beautiful, only when one paints something one cannot see with one's eyes.

March 25, 1989

The stroke has no starting point, no centre, no last portion.

Russian icons are painted more carefully than Chagall's paintings, but Chagall's works are truer.

March 31, 1989

The figures follow the directions suggested by the eggshell.

Polish until the lines are scraped off, destroy all ancient forms of eggshell, then tie them up.

Constantly demolish the shapes that appear, demolishing the shapes doesn't mean adding new shapes.

Reduce more, constantly reduce, let the lines be scraped off again, continually scraped off so that the eggshell, expected to be beautiful, can remain.

The position of the figure must be firm. One must

411

weigh the pros and the cons of the degree of heaviness and lightness and of the equilibrium, the tower shape creates firmness.

A sketch is only an anticipation of the painting. When gluing the eggshells, one has to follow the eggshell's inclination, as well as the one of the lacquer to develop.

The classical look is plain and firm. As for Chagall's world, it's completely different.

It isn't sure yet that it's good, when one succeeds accordingly to one's intention. Just close one's eyes and go ahead, and one often actually succeeds.One must have a great confidence to start ahead with closed eyes.

Scraped off, scraped off again, then join again.

Wishing to found a high-leveled art gallery or a low-leveled one, means one's already partial.

April 14, 1989

No analyzing, no arguing, and while dividing the "void-ness' one also obtains an emptiness.

The painting seems to form itself, one doesn't have to intervene in it.

Searching and creating is like planting trees, one turns up the big root and can make the tree thriving but can also make it wither. It would be safer to dig a small hole and let the water permeate little by little.

The "existing" is nay, the" non-existing" is also nay.

In all sentimental aspects, weeping is the most complete one. One weeps when one's sad, one also weeps when one's happy. Weeping heals the breach between all sentiments. When one can no longer weep, it means that everything is exhausted in oneself.

One must be the thing that can see everything.

One doesn't have to groove the eggshells, all figures and forms already exist in the interstices. One only needs to plaster with paint.

Working on tiny details, one has to understand them to have good effect. Otherwise, it would be useless whether one works or not.

One cannot escape as one is still a bit dotty, and greedy.

Upon practicing religion, one brings along a series of people.Were one to succeed to escape,they'll also be able to break free.

May 5, 1989

What one ties up oneself is the real deliverance, there is nothing sure in life, there is only the work one is doing that is sure.

While going one thinks that's a deliverance, but actually one is tying up oneself tighter.

The change that strongly hits one from outside is the real change. Were one to assume so, it'll be only a false change.

Keep the new, the sharpness from being dusty. Boldness causes the strokes to be tightened.

Apprehensiveness creates futility.

At the beginning, one ought to make things murky, later one can rectify them easily.

What one can do is thanks to God, thanks to geniuses that give one tips.

Gluing the gold is important in the fact that gold leaves tuck at the edges of figures.

Literature also assists.

414

High-levelled literature and poetry and painting art aren't against one another.

Art and beauty contain everything within them: thought, philosophy, religion etc ....
All unintentional things that turn into success are good.

In life as well as in art, things happen in such or such way because one states the question in an important manner, otherwise, it'll be like a wafting wind.

Apprehensiveness and watchfulness cause the painting to be inconsequent and futile. Boldness allies everything into a sole block.

Painting is like bonzes practicing religion, each achieved work is a mutation.

August 14, 1989

One has to prepare oneself for working on a bigger project to be able to realize a smaller one. Were one to work only on small things, one'll not be able to work on great things. A failed great work starts from many small failures.

One has to overcome many impossibilities. Each painter has his own limits.

Producing means sailing on the Wisdom boat (Prajna), and one has to let it take one to wherever it wants.

With an abstract painting, it seems like one is encaging a herd of animals altogether. The figures, strokes, colours, substances ... are multitudinous and completely different from one another, and only one's *"gentle mind"* can pull them together, forming a unique block.

Mr. I once looked at my paintings and asked me: "How come your paintings have a primitive nature, while you've never gone abroad to look at paintings in museums?".[1]

Art must have some primitive nature to be everlasting.

Were one to turn into air, then maybe one'll be less

---

(1) Sebartes asked Picasso about primitive art he said: "Primitive sculpture has never been surpassed. Have you noticed the precision of the lines engraved in the caverns?... You have seen reproductions... The Assyrian bas-reliefs still keep a similar purity of expression".
"How do you explain to yourself", I asked, "the disappearance of this marvelous simplicity?".
"This is due to the fact that man ceased to be simple. He wanted to see farther and so he lost the faculty of understanding that which he had within the reach of his vision. When one reflects, one pauses. I do not mean to say that one stops along the way while walking, but that one's machinery breaks down, and once this happens it is the end. If you balance yourself at the brink of an abyss you'll fall..." (Sebartés, 1948, page 213).

unfortunate. Air itself is also unfortunate, when it's rainy and windy, air turns ghastly pale ....

It's quite ordinary that some aged persons continue to be stupid.

November 23, 1989

Lacquer is a substance that can hardly be mechanized.

Painting means being constantly dissatisfied, and permanently widening one's sphere.

Painting of the type "The fall of Icarus" [1] is more difficult than Chagall's paintings. But, with Picasso, his paintings are similar to Icarus' Fall. One has to fall one time to acquire a habit.

The true and the false share a unique character.

With lacquer, one just go ahead and work and it'll change itself.

Question: Do you feel weary while looking at ancient sketches you've drawn?
Aswer: No, they look like newly drawn.

November 29, 1989

Upon "feeling" something, one has to work accordingly to that feeling. All steps shall be decided at that moment, without foreseeing any "method".

The painting can be sensed, depending on the level of each individual.

People don't like the "solitary walker". Kind of wicked person.

Question: "Is it true that while living in plenty, man is more "virtuous"?
Answer: That's a false "virtue". Man is extremely wicked.

Buddha doesn't want his "doctrine" to be interrupted, and wants to preach it to the world everlastingly.

January 9, 1990

Poetry doesn't need elaboration. Painting is like poetry and needs some elaboration, but unintentionally.

Question: What's the purpose of poetry?
Answer: Such a question is superfluous.

Once wearied one even doesn't want to remove an eyelash that sticks to one's eye.

418

January 24, 1990

The tiny obsessions will end when one goes far away. Exterior things cannot effect one's inner self.

Question: In the sutras the term "layman" is often used, what does "layman" mean?
Answer: A thing.

Question: How gilding is proceeded?
Answer: I don't know, I'm as blind as you. Don't get into what I've done.

At first, gild that "unidentified thing". "Satisfaction with one's lot" and "Permanent dissatisfaction" are one.

Creating is at first a made- up story, then it becomes true. Paint whatever one wants, there's no obligation at all.

April, 1990

While gilding, one doesn't need any change, both straight look and tilted look are beautiful.

In painting, to reach good results, one has to be quick, otherwise it'll addle. Mr. I. also has a similar idea.

May 1990

Enthusiasm causes the paintiing to be fresh and cool.

One must have strength to work in a stretch. The entirety will come together, otherwise it will disintegrate.

The space of oil paintings breaks off while the space of lacquer congeals.[1]

June 1990

The lacquer and vermilion must be pressed to become steady.

Discussing freely the question is also good, however it makes everything confused.

Some people don't have an unruffled mind to read through a page, some read then later on forget all about, a fortiori composing and reciting poems or explaining the texts.

---

(1) One has to work on lacquers for a very long time to be able to perceive this fact. A lacquer might be painted in a very long time, with many layers, and with an unbounded pressing force on the painting.

Were one to say prayers only, it would be difficult to enter the kingdom of God.

Working in lacquer, one must know how to exploit the unforeseen matters that occur all by themselves.

Question: Why have you stopped painting?
Answer: Being able to paint or not doesn't depend on myself.

One has to be natural in order to become supernatural later on.

Natural and soft is good.

Upon saying *"simple but elaborate"*, one already perceives some sluggishness. Arguments are resembling one another. It would be good only when not even one word is left.[1]

A dreamy state is the most concentrated one. Even the slightest idea causes one to be impeded. One must change to have the "new".

Not dealing with ignorance is already thorough.

Enjoying literature and admiring occidental art don't

_____

(1) Then he added: "I even don't care about writing".

lead to entire satisfaction.

While creating, one has to lean on ancient things, as the things one is doing oneself are quite weak.

One becomes old again when looking for the "new".

Question: The rhythm of music, the modern films, do they have a relation with our creative works?
Answer: No, but at times, they cause us to be impeded.

Looking at a painting, one sees that its lay-out isn't steady yet, this is because when looking too close to it, one doesn't see the entirety. Getting deeply into details causes the entirety to be weakened.

Creative work requires continuity.

Painting lacquer so as to discover its rhythm of life.

January 31, 1992

Poetry comforts people a great deal.

One can learn a lot from literature.

May 6, 1992

422

One must look for the joint of everything.

Only by working on big paintings can one batter down one's old habits.

Is there anything impeding in one's style? It would be more slippery if dry. Pure and clean is nothing more than a mere vocable.

While painting, does one feel true or illusive?

Question: Where can one get one's strength when one relinquishes everything, even one's passion?
Answer: One must look for a source of strength.

Working in lacquer, when one lets it rest   is when one meditates.

One must "*see*" to be able to achieve beauty.

CONCLUSION

Since 1979, each time I achieve a lacquer painting, I always brought it to artist Nguyễn Gia Trí, submitting it to his appreciation, and in quest of his advice and observations.

The greatest one is the one entitled: "Sight of the Lake of the Returned Sword", sizes: 0.80 x 2.40 metres.

Four or five month before his death, along with the down-grade of the lacquer painting art, due to the fact that no one understands its intrinsic value, and also due to the fact that there were no buyers, the sizes of the lacquer paintings I've realized began to shrink.

I've had to show him lacquers as small as a hand or half of a hand.

He composedly said: "Our time is over" [1]

I asked him: "We, means yourself, or both you and I?". He kept silence and didn't answer.

*

---

(1) It seems that he used to adopt Lao-Ji's irrational way of speaking such as: when wishing someone to be stronger, drown him and make him weaker.

I once said: "When our nation develops and turns richer, the lacquer painting art will develop" – he only said: "sometimes until one dies, one still cannot sell any painting"

One or two months before his dead, each time when I visited him, he always remained completely silent, looking at me with a gaze that seems that I'm not a stranger for him, but at the same time I'm unknown to him...

Previously, there was a short period of time in which I saw that he weakened very much. I told him: "I'm too ignorant, you've shown me many things which I still cannot see".

He said: "It's my fault".

This note-keeping book is made available today after 17 years, through which I've been keeping notes of all his words, and I've submitted to him, leaving it with him for about one or two weeks. He doesn't have any idea about it, and I wonder whether he had read it or not?

There was only a unique time in which he had a vague insinuation: "We're far ahead of other people, they'll have to interpret us".

Twenty days before the day he passed away, I came to visit him for the last time, he lay silently on the bed and used his hands to sign to me: shut the ears,shut the eyes, shut the lips, then he put his forefinger at the centre of his forehead.

May 1, 1995
In commemoration of the 2ᵈ anniversary of the
death of painter Nguyễn Gia Trí
Nguyễn Xuân Việt

LACQUER PAINTING

By painter Tô Ngọc Vân

Since the years 30's of this century, with the re searches and experimentations of several artists from the first generation, from a decorative and handicraft branch, lacquer has become day after day an actual plastic art substance. But the position of lacquer hadn't been immediately asserted. In the first years of the resistance war against the French colonialists, filled with great hardships and distress, many artists – the most typical one was Tô Ngọc Vân – through their creative works and arguments – had continued to affirm the plastic art position of lacquer painting.

In the Nationwide Cultural Congress at Việt Bắc in 1948, painter Tô Ngọc Vân had given a lecture on lacquer. Later on, the text had been published on the Literature and Arts magazine, issue No. 5 (September, 1948). This is an important literary dissertation affirming the position and the great capacity of lacquer painting. In spite of the rarity of documents and information of the resistance, and although, there are a few ideas that might be considered as not worthing the trouble, compared with the present time's situation, the affirmations of the author have been proven by time and by the development of lacquer painting.

As we're preparing to commemorate the 45th anniversary of the publishing of the first issue of the Literary and Art magazine, we wish to present hereafter artist Tô Ngọc Vân's article as a whole:

The term SON MÀI (lacquer) is a new term that has been used only a few years ago to designate a technique formerly called SON TA (traditional Vietnamese paint), that has been entirely transformed due to the paint polishing art.

The traditional Vietnamese paint technique is similar to the one of Chinese paint. Legend has it that the Chinese paint existed since the Han dynasty, using like the traditional Vietnamese paint a type of material called live paint. In our country, this type of live paint exists and is produced in large quantities at Phú Thọ, and used to be sold to China and Japan.

Since 1931 and previously, the use of traditional Vietnamese paint, like the one of Chinese paint in China, and Japanese paint in Japan, consisted of coating and covering various objects to make them radiantly beautiful; these were ordinary daily use things such as a tray, a casket, a pair of wooden shoes... or worshipping objects such as altars, platforms for holding bowls and plates ... or decorative items such as parallel sentences, frontispiece and distiches, screens... with various colours such as:vermilion,black, red brown, gold, silver, according to established traditions. Plainly speaking, traditional Vietnamese paint was used only for decorative works, and its place was only within the decorative art. Although in Japan, the painting art was the most refined one, but none of the countries had thought of conducting research works and using the paint material in any other way different with the traditional one, or venturing in the paint art to look for a means to increase the artistic quality of traditional paint, by means of inventing its additional abilities.

Starting from the year 1931, on the occasion of the International Fair in Paris, the Vietnamese artists had wanted to displayed there art works bearing Vietnamese national characteristics, and for that purpose, they had used traditional Vietnamese paint as a plastic art means to produce a few paintings. Examining those works, one perceived the intention to liberate traditional Vietnamese paint from its decorative condition, but some hesitation was still involved, and no decision was taken. Although the style had been different and the mixing of colours had differed from the traditional one, the technique remained that of paint for trays, for caskets. Actually, those works had not been able to move the paint substance any inch from its original condition. Is it true that these artists had been hesitating because the question seemed too important and great for them, as it was question of altering the course of a two thousand years old technique.

But from 1931 and later on, thanks to the dedicated researches of a number of talented artists that gave up oil paint to specialize themselves in traditional Vietnamese paint, our traditional paint had been able to liberate itself from the place it was imprisoned to deliberately advance on the strange and immense plastic arts horizon. From a casket, a pair of wooden shoes, it has cleared all obstacles to become a precious framed art work; from a supplementary means used for increasing the beauty of objects, it has turned into an independent means, capable of depicting the artist's soul, a prosperous means that

428

even domineered OIL PAINT. Forgetting its past, the traditional Vietnamese paint changed its modest name into that of LACQUER PAINTING.

Noticing the recent appearance of LACQUER PAINTING, the majority of the Vietnamese artist's circle received it with open arms. They saw in LACQUER PAINTING a technique, created by Vietnamese, that quite suits our nation's climate. Foreigners visiting our country completely welcomed LACQUER PAINTING, considering it as a newest invention in the plastic arts, and they warmly encouraged it.

But, there were also a number of French colonialists that, upon seeing that our traditional paint had just quit its decorative condition, had hastily shouted: "Stop!" The daily Volonté Indochinoise (Indochinese Will) had declared that: "TRADITIONAL VIETNAMESE PAINT shouldn't and couldn't take the plastic arts path, it shouldn't because it was serving effectively the decorative art, why take it to another place; and it couldn't as its poor means and insufficient colours cannot be used effectively to depict all creatures in an accurate way. Right at that time, on a newspaper, we have discussed about those unstable reasoning already. And the lacquer works, displayed before the public since 1935 up to now, have demonstrated that LACQUER PAINTING, adopting the plastic arts path, has been taking the right path, as plastic arts is not aimed at recopying creatures, but it specializes itself in depicting the interior life of the artist, just like Chinese ink painting or modern world Oil painting.

Today, after having observed and keeping track with Lacquer

429

Painters, and after having experimented ourselves for a certain length of time, we can confidently declare that: lacquer painting has been not only a branch of plastic arts, but it's also a branch of plastic arts that has enough capacity to revolutionize the world plastic arts that is now in an impasse. That's the point I wish to present to the Congress. Please let me cite concrete data:

At first, let's take into consideration the history of OIL PAINT which is typical of today's world plastic arts. Originating from Europe, it has been spread to China and Japan over one hundred years ago, and has reached Vietnam 20 years ago; OIL PAINT is the most perfect means to materialize realistic art in painting, and is a branch of painting well appreciated by all modern countries in the world, and for that reason, it has been internationalized.

Since the flourishing Italian Renaissance time, OIL PAINT had continually advanced towards realism, its target. Studying human anatomy and searching on the law of perspective, were essential elements that increased that capacity of plastic arts, helping it to reach the stage of depicting all creatures in a completely accurate way. When photography, a scientific means for drawing a likeness was invented, OIL PAINT that was on the path of realism had stopped. Seeing that realism, its target, had been reached by photography, plastic arts hesitated and wanted to switch to another direction. But, towards what direction?

From this moment and in the preceding time, painters from everywhere looked towards Italy and considered the arts of RAPHAEL, MICHELANGELO, LEONARDO da VINCI as the zenith of plas-

430

tic arts, and found there a vital source for their own works, a source which today has turned old and no longer suits it. According to CAMILLE MAUCLAIR, the German philosophers, at that same time, had declared that: "The Occident had drawn, till exhaustion, all the essence of Latinism, to look for new vital strength, the Occident must turn towards Asia. This situation took place towards the end of the 19th century. Amid that perplexed atmosphere, the Goncourt brothers had, for the first time, introduced to the European public a number of Japanese wood engravings. As soon as these engravings appeared, the plastic arts immediately saw its new vital source. Then, a revolution occurred, taking the plastic arts out of its former framework, leading it towards a new path, on which it went from attending to realism only to a certain degree to no longer attending to realism at all, and reaching surrealism as it is now. On its way, the starting point was represented by Manet (French painter), and the stage it's resting now is represented by Salvador Dali (Spanish painter), passing through Gauguin, Matisse (French painters), Chagall (Russian painter), Van Gogh (Dutch painter), and Picasso (Spanish painter). The prestige of the new school is quite illustrious, and its influence spreads from West to East, as far as Japan and also to Vietnam until the recent World War.

But, even in its victorious days, this painting school, called by people "LIVING PAINTING" had carried with it the germ of its destruction. This is because it has been running around the vicious circle represented by Manet, Dali, without succeeding to escape from it.

The above – mentioned artists only trained smaller Manet, reduce-in-sizes Picasso, or tiny Van Gogh. The painters have been fed up with Oil paint, and found that it's incapable of serving the creativity of plastic arts, accordingly to the requirements of the new art. Picasso himself have had to mix sand to OIL PAINT to transform OIL PAINT into another substance. Instead of using the paint brush, one has painted with one's fingers, with a brush, with a knife, to give to the painting a new quality. But whatever the direction OIL PAINT is rotated to, one continues to feel dissatisfied. And after 50 years of transformation, oil paint falls again in a puzzled state like the one towards the end of the last century, while it no longer knows where to find new vital strength, and thus is again in an impasse. The European opinion seems to ask itself: to where, should the painting art be oriented?

We answered: towards Vietnam!
World painting, in our opinion, will find its resurrection in LAC-QUER PAINTING.

The radiant constitution of LACQUER can satisfy the artist's aspiration to look for a new substance, pleasing to the eye, and more emotional than OIL PAINT. The substances of red brown, of black, gold and silver in LACQUER PAINTING are so lively, and are no longer a soulless substance.

The colours of LACQUER PAINTING are deeply affection-ate, their shades are resounding deeply, causing the heart – of – heart – of the viewer to vibrate. None of the red colours of OIL PAINT,could avoid being quite pale when placed beside the vermilion of LACQUER PAINTING. None of the black colour of OIL PAINT, could avoid

432

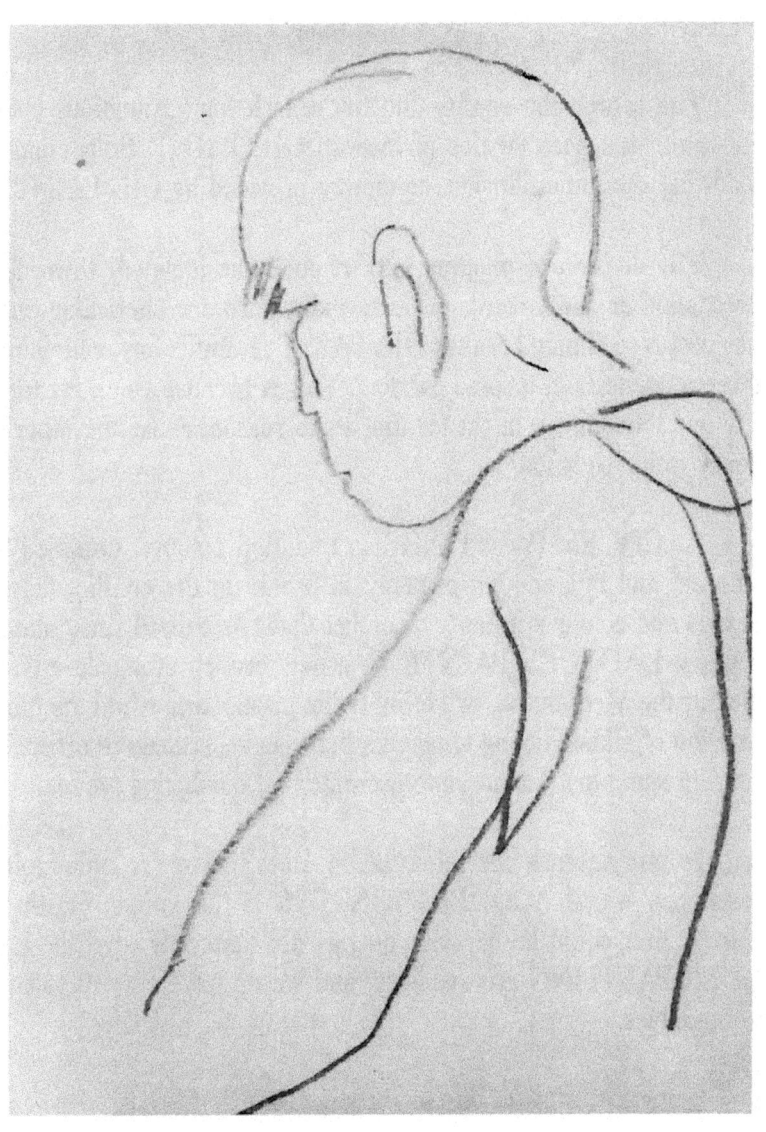

"Họa sĩ Nguyễn Gia Trí trong xưởng vẽ" ký họa của Nguyễn Xuân Việt
"Artist Nguyễn Gia Trí inside his studio" sketch by artist Nguyễn Xuân Việt

being faded and jaunty when placed beside the black colour of LAC-QUER.

The search for quality and the search for harmonious colours constitute the peculiarities of modern OIL PAINT. Both elements, following the initial illusion, cannot be provided by OIL PAINT.

The division of painters into schools: one inclined towards figures, another one towards colours, and a third one cherishing quality, has occurred simply because OIL PAINT is unfit for containing all three tendencies in a same painting. This is because when it can satisfy one tendency, it might for that same reason, cause the other tendency to be excluded.

LACQUER PAINTING has qualified colours, qualified substances, and has enough capacity to break up the conflict between figures and colour substances, conflict that has existed since almost a century. LACQUER PAINTING, a new branch of plastic arts, created by the Vietnamese, will bring to the plastic arts world the harmonization of all conflicting tendances that had separated the artists, that share a same lust for life, into separate and conflicting groups.

In our nation's special situation, in which we're undergoing a resistance war, LACQUER PAINTING is the unique plastic art activity that could be carried out, as the materials used for LAC-QUER PAINTING are available, and we do have enough to supply to ourselves.

Being interrupted, due to the disorders that occurred when we

433

first started our war of resistance, LACQUER PAINTING now can operate again. The studies, aimed at perfecting the LACQUER techniques have been resumed.

The longer our war of resistance is, the more we'll have time to bring LACQUER PAINTING to the utmost BEAUTY, so that at our first minute of independence, LACQUER PAINTING will be fashioned by the Vietnamese, and will serve as a souvenir sent by people that had fought for liberty and peace to artists throughout the world, thus contributing our people's part to the task of building new LETTERS AND ARTS for mankind.

(Briefing made before the Nationwide Cultural Congress 1948)

TÔ NGỌC VÂN - THE ARTIST PAINTER WHO SEES THROUGH AND THROUGH 100 YEARS

By Nguyễn Xuân Việt

In 1948, in the first days of the war of resistance against the french colonialists that were full of hardship at the nation-wide cultural Congress in Việt Bắc, painter Tô Ngọc Vân has put forth his appraisal of the lasting value of lacquer painting: "European opinion worried about the fact: to where world painting should direct itself? We answered: toward Vietnam. In our opinion, world painting will find a way to restore itself to life in our lacquer painting".

For what reason, artist Tô Ngọc Vân, one among the few people that throughly understand the lacquer material and that belong in the Indochina school of Fine Arts, has discovered in lacquer painting the capacity to "restore world painting to life" To understand his appraisal that sees through and through a hundred years, we ought to go back to the years and months that have seen the birth of artistic lacquer,then place it in the Vietnamese cultural framework in relation with the panorama of world art and culture at that time.

From the 16th to the 19th century, Christianism came to Vietnam through many itineraries, creating conditions to form the Romanized Vietnamese language replacing the Chinese characters and the Nôm (Demotic characters). At the middle of the 19th century, the french colonialists invaded Vietnam. Along with such facts figures the meeting between french and vietnamese cultures. All such factors have created great and sudden cultural and social changes in Vietnam. In my personal opinion, Oriental and Western cultures have chosen for themselves their most solid combination and connection point on this very land. It's a certainty that from the middle of the 19th century to the beginning of the 40's in the 20th century, Vietnam is the land on which occurs the strongest and most complete cultural interference in mankind's cultural history. And this is the mingling and sticking between the french culture, originating from greek and roman cultures, and the vietnamese culture which is derived from indian and chinese sources with their traditional Confucean, Taoist and Buddhist thought that have had thousands of years of development. All such ancient thoughts have turned into the main life-line that tends our national culture.

Casting a look back to the cultural works, the paintings and music of this stage, we can see that it's also the very period of time in which are born new standards, bearing the classical face of contemporary vietnamese culture.

With the painting art, we've had special particular

new steps. *Vietnam is one of the two important destinations of the artistic itinerary towards the begingning of the 20th century which had its source from Paris, the world art capital. The first itinerary led to America since the beginning of the 30's, following the steps of European great artists who came to America as war refugees, and constituted the main factor that gave birth to the New York school. The second itinerary led to Vietnam through the founding of the Indo-China school of Fine Arts in 1925. For that reason, upon approaching the western art for the first time, the vietnamese artists have used the world plastic art language that continued almost 600 years of european plastic art, through the oil international material. They have had the change to study and conduct researches together in a College taught by talented, professional, and conscientious french masters. The plastic art concepts they had adopted at that time was quite early and new when compared with all countries outside of Europe. The new plastic art works were not easily received and accepted if not guided by really talented masters. Let's listen to Pollock, a great artist painter from the New York school who said in 1944: "I must recognize that the masterworks in these recent 100 years have been painted in France, a majority of american artists don't understand anything about new paintings... For that reason, the presence of renowned European artists here is very important as they have brought about a throughout understanding of the new plastic artworks".*

In Vietnam, under the guidance of artist V. TARDIEU and master J. INGUIMBERTY, the artists from the Indo-China school of Fine Arts have throughly understood the European classical and contemporary plastic arts. They understood and used oil paint just like their contemporary European professional artists, but the oil paint simply doesn't not satisfied the vietnamese painters' profound oriental soul. Artist painter J. INGUIMBERTY, the teacher so close to them, also hopes to discover "the new" when coming to Indo-China. The Eastern and Western spirit and heart have met like a communion and a continuity of mankind's intellect from West to East. The vietnamese artists, through the guidance and encouragement of their masters, have gone through oil paint to discover lacquer painting. Concerning this matter, we ought to mention artist Trần Quang Trân's merit, when he went to Japan to study lacquer and brought back a certain number of traditionnal lacquer techniques.

The french master COURBET, in one of his articles on art has had an essential word on creativity: "Art doesn't begin with a zero, it goes from conclusion to conclusion". While painter Nguyễn Sáng also voiced another harsh law in art: "Art doesn't have a second class, it's either gold or brass". This is because the nature of painting is directly related to eternity, just like with music, the beautifulness doesn't need any translation, but, different with music, painting has no intermediary. Painting has an advantage over all other forms of cultures and arts, as it doesn't get any obstruction brought about by externalities, the painter, while creating, gets in touch directly and completely with the tangible world as well as the metaphysical world by means of his mission to transform the inanimate material into a spiritual beauty. Throughout his life, a real artist only leaves behind paintings which, upon reaching the art summit in painting, have reached an eternal life and obtained a great value vis-à-vis the whole world. Is it the reason why, E. POWELL, the Curator of the American National Museum has remarked: "The expressionist elements and the artistic methods have cause Art to become Man's principal experiences".

Today, the more we look back at the panorama of 100 years of World Art, the more we feel that we're treasuring the lacquer material. In the effervescent 20th century of plastic arts, the Asian artists living on their own homeland are completely absent, only a few Asian artists' names are mentioned, while almost all of them are living abroad, as they are living and creating in Europe and America for quite a long time. This fact shows the difficulty of art and the importance of materials used. In days past, in the 16th and 18th centuries, only with wood engraving, Japan has had a series of world-stature artists, and has also awakened the french impressionists, causing them to know how to look at painting with new eyes. But, in the 20th century, the main vitality of world painting was oil painting. Asian painting must have its thousand years old local material to em-

439

body itself and create its traditional and eerie Oriental spiritual beauty. And the vietnamese artists, with their sharp creative intuition and with only 10 years of study under the french masters, have for the first time presented the Exhibition of Artistic Lacquers in HaNoi in 1935.

From that "marvellous first time" up to now, Vietnamese lacquer is already almost 70 years old, a period of time not short at all nowadays. Vietnamese art has created a change in the question of material for the world plastic art. This is a fire lighted by the thousand-year-old Oriental beauty upon adopting the western plastic art essence and the oriental traditional lacquer technique of Japan.

But upon comparing with oil painting which has almost 600 years of age, we can see that artistic lacquer painting is still too young, too new, and has not yet been summed up to permit people to realize its great intrinsic value. In days past, artist Tô Ngọc Vân must have the genius and a great confidence, and he also must know himself and understand other people to dare to conclude: "We do believe and dare to declare that lacquer painting is not only a branch of plastic art, but it also has the ability to revolutionize world painting which is in an impass". A world cultural researcher has had the following remark some 40 years ago: "The synthesis of East and West, which is the basis of mankind's genuineness, is a matter of life and death and is maybe the most urgent problem of nowadays" G.M. HERZEN. With the *artistic lacquer painting, Vietnam has achieved the said East and West synthesis. The cultural prejudices, the shallowness in performing researching works, and particularly the lack of self-confidence and the utterly foreign inclined mind of a number of painters and arguers have prevented us from seeing and realizing the greatness which vietnamese culture has reached with artistic lacquer painting.*

Through the masterpieces by painters representatives of the Indo-China school of Fine Arts, we do have a whole treasure, an illuminating bloc of pearl with our lacquer painting to contribute to the common culture of mankind. From such masterpieces, we run into the thousand-year-old spiritual line of Vietnam which is chrystallized and is expressed today. This is a very important matter as, from such contemporary masterpieces bearing mankind's new value, upon catching the light of other cultural creations, we will perceive the whole panorama, the whole cultural source of our nation. This is an eternal source of life, implicating no beginning and no ending. Reaching this NATIONAL AND HUMANISTIC depth, vietnamese culture then will reach genuine freedom. It also liberates itself from western means and techniques it had had to borrow initially, and finally vietnamese culture is liberating itself from its seamy sides that are binding, obstructing and concealing its creative source. Seamy sides that prevents our creativeness to reach the universal value of mankind as a whole.

Talking about artistic lacquer painting, many

futuristic generations will still think of artist painter Tô Ngọc Vân. One of the world-size intellectuals with a century overcrossing vision so rare in Vietnam, artist Tô Ngọc Vân was killed in the Điện Biên Phủ campaign like a fighter fighting for the freedom of our nation. His debate on "lacquer painting", though voiced and written more than half of a century ago, still for ever encourages and awakens the today's creative people.

Article written on the occasion of the 100th birth anniversary of painter Tô Ngọc Vân
Nguyễn Xuân Việt
Translated by Vũ Anh Tuấn

Sai Gon 24-01-60

A LETTER OF PAINTER NGUYỄN GIA TRÍ
ADDRESSED TO PAINTER PHẠM TĂNG

Dear Phạm Tăng,

Today all employees in my studio have taken their leaves for Tết, leaving me free so I am writing to ask after your health. How are you and how is you studying?

Have you paid Mr. I.a visit? When seeing him, please send him my regards.

Living there you would see that it is not the painters' works and their styles that we have seen would have the best effect that lasts long on us. In my opinion, the art of painting abroad is not like ours in our homeland. Ours has too much falsity and empty bearing. In such countries like France or Italia, people have their traditional groove to follow. Their good, for my money, is that they really seek something and they have a kind of belief. I don't mean the belief implying that arts were a kind of religion, like some amateur painters may have seen arts as a very trite form of religion.

I am sure that you have met painters whether they are of the most weird "surrealism" or "abstractionism". If they are true painters, you will see them very common and simple, because it is natural that they are so. Sometime ago I bought a copy of Art d'Aujourd'hui in which there are pictures of new American and Italian artworks. Some of them look fine, but I don't know how they will really look if I see them live. If reading their articles you may see that besides cryptic theories, the rest sounds rather "literary" that could make us doubtful of the matter. Chances are that they may have made some scientific or philosophical experiments, and nothing else. But those are necessary experiments; of course there may be one amongst tens of thousands of people to be lucky enough to find a diamond. I admire their courage.

Nguyễn Gia Trí
Translated by Nguyễn Huỳnh Điệp

MỤC LỤC

HỌA SĨ NGUYỄN GIA TRÍ NÓI VỀ SÁNG TẠO
NGUYỄN XUÂN VIỆT - Ghi lại

NHÀ XUẤT BẢN VĂN NGHỆ
179 Lý Chính Thắng, Quận 3, TP. HCM - ĐT: (08) 9316435 -
5260124 - 8249528 - Fax: (08) 9316435 - Email: nxbvannghe@vnn.vn

Chịu trách nhiệm xuất bản:	NGUYỄN ĐỨC BÌNH
Biên tập:	THANH PHƯỢNG
Sửa bản in:	AN - PHÁT
Bìa:	NGUYỄN ANH CƯƠNG

(Phụ bản tranh sơn mài Nguyễn Gia Trí của nhà
thờ dòng Đa Minh và nhà sưu tập Trần Hậu Tuấn)

PAINTER NGUYỄN GIA TRÍ'S WORDS ON CREATION
Notes kept by NGUYỄN XUÂN VIỆT

Responsible for publishing:	NGUYỄN ĐỨC BÌNH
Editor:	THANH PHƯỢNG
Corrector:	AN - PHÁT
Presentation and cover:	NGUYỄN ANH CƯƠNG
Translator:	VŨ ANH TUẤN
Plates by	NGUYỄN XUÂN VIỆT

In lần thứ I, số lượng: 1.000 cuốn, khổ 14,5 x 20,5cm. Tại Xí nghiệp in FAHASA.
Số đăng ký KHXB: 70-2009/CXB/139-01/VNTPHCM. QĐXB số: 326/QĐ-
NXBVN. Ký ngày 31 tháng 12 năm 2009. In xong và nộp lưu chiểu 2010.